COMING HOME
to MYSELF

COMING HOME
to MYSELF

*Reflections for Nurturing a
Woman's Body and Soul*

MARION WOODMAN and JILL MELLICK

WATERCOLOR PAINTINGS by JILL MELLICK

CONARI PRESS
Berkeley, CA

Conari Press books are distributed by Publishers Group West

Cover Design: Evelyn C. Shapiro
Cover Illustration: Pamela Becker, Sacred Moon Studio
Cover Art Direction: Ame Beanland
Book Design: Suzanne Albertson

ISBN: 1-57324-100-8

Library of Congress Cataloging-in-Publication Data

Woodman, Marion.
Coming home to myself : daily reflections for a woman's
body and soul / Marion Woodman and Jill Mellick.
p.   cm.
ISBN: 1-573240100-8 (hardcover)
1. Women—Conduct of life. 2. Meditation.
I. Mellick, Jill. II. Title.
BJ1610.W66   1998   98-10067
158.1'28'082—dc21   CIP

Printed in the United States of America on recycled paper
3   5   7   9   10   8   6   4   2

To: SOPHIA

To our ShaSha sisters

To the vast community of women
who are loving their femininity,
themselves and each other

To the vast community of men
who are coming to grips with the lost
feminine in themselves.

—M.W.

and

And for Tara, Paloma, Ariana, Amiya, Povi,
and those who stand on the threshold.

—J.M.

Coming Home to Myself

ix

Linearity does not come naturally
to me. It kills my imagination.
Nothing happens.

No bell rings.
No moment of here and now.
No moment that says yes.
Without these, I am not alive.

I prefer the pleasure
of the journey through the spiral.

Relax.
Enjoy the spiral.
If you miss something
on the first round,
don't worry.
You might pick it up
on the second—or third—or ninth.
It doesn't matter.

Relax.
Timing is everything.
If the bell does ring,
it will resonate
through all the rungs of your spiral.
If it doesn't ring,
it is the wrong spiral—
or the wrong time—
or there is no bell.

1

New Resonances

MARION WOODMAN

Coming Home to Myself is a surprise child. Born of the insight of my friend and colleague, Jill Mellick, and my growing curiosity as we revisioned my earlier work, this little book has happened. Our editor, Mary Jane Ryan, dared the intuitive leap that is re-birthing my work in a distilled form.

I began writing my journal when I was twelve. I am still writing because I am compelled to find meaning in my experience. In my late teens, I chose to sacrifice my beloved microscope for another kind of poetry, the poetry of word. Still, the scientist in me is always observing with a thinking heart, noting, comparing, articulating.

Twenty years ago, much to my surprise, people were interested in my thesis on eating disorders. Being an addict myself and profoundly introverted, I was fearful of publication. With the encouragement of Inner City Books, the thesis was revised and published as *The Owl Was a Baker's Daughter.*

Addiction to Perfection was my first attempt at writing a book. It came out of an inner drive to understand the repetitive themes in the dreams of my addicted clients. I put rows of dreams on the floor of my studio, organized and reorganized them by theme. I marveled at the overwhelming power of the unconscious and, at the same time, the intensity of its drive toward healing.

One theme became clear as I began work on *The Pregnant Virgin.* The way to healing an addiction lies in finding a connection between body and soul. Soul needs body as much as body needs soul. Each is out of context without the other, an abandoned fragment of what it is. A great cherishing mother is often the link that manifests in dreams. Sometimes she appears as a striding Presence in the sky, sometimes as a bigger-than-life cleaning lady or a down-to-earth crone. She has many names: Buffalo Woman, Black Madonna, Isis, Anna, Tara. In the Bible she is called Wisdom, translated from the Greek word, *Sophia.* Whatever her temporal form, she is divine; she understands our humanity and her love is fierce enough to permeate flesh and bone. Her humor rips away veils of illusion. She is the central figure in *Dancing in the Flames,*

(Shambhala, 1996) which I co-authored with my friend, Elinor Dickson.

As I watched the pregnant virgin coming to consciousness in dreams, I became increasingly alarmed by images of ravaged masculinity, masculinity and femininity both being ravaged by patriarchy. Men and women who have worked hard to find a strong feminine standpoint in Being are now working hard to release a masculinity strong enough to partner the evolving virgin consciousness. This theme began by exploring the tragedy of perfection as Keats' "unravished bride" in "Ode on a Grecian Urn." So the process went on through *The Ravaged Bridegroom, Conscious Femininity,* and *Leaving My Father's House.*

One thing has been distilled in my consciousness. By whatever name we call the two magnets that create this balance of energies in our bodies and in our planet— Masculine/Feminine, Shiva/Shakti, Yang/Yin, Spirit/Soul, Transcendence/Immanence, Doing/Being, we are now responsible for making space for the healing of body, soul, and spirit. We are being directed in the evolutionary process by divine guides through our dreams, our symptoms, our planet. New values are emerging—feminine values and masculine values that are free of patriarchal abuse. A totally new harmonic lies ahead in the new millennium.

I write this down not because I am trying to sell my books, but because, as an intuitive, I tend to take too

4

much for granted—I fail to fill in the facts that would make my thinking clear. As my husband says as he walks past my studio door, "You're not a born writer, Marion. Every time I walk by, you're gazing at the trees. You think everything through and then you write down your conclusion. A born writer would keep writing the process down."

He is right. People who are not intuitive become frustrated trying to follow my unstated logic and sensation types throw up their hands or the book in alarm when they feel their body responding but not their mind. I try to put down the facts, but I think in images, so when I try to explain, I end up in another image, which only compounds the difficulty. Moreover, my mind is a tapestry of the many great writers whom I have studied all my life. Their imagery is the warp and woof of my own thinking.

As a professor and practitioner of psychotherapy and the creative arts, Jill has worked from my books for many years. As she says in her introduction, she has taken my books and "has allowed the armature, the bones of the writing to show through the transparent skin of the prose and emphasized the closely interwoven relationships between images or thoughts by reflecting their relationship in their syntax." Her own book, *The Natural Artistry of Dreams* (Conari Press, 1996), with its wealth of creative ideas for releasing the energy of dream imagery, is a splendid companion text for this book.

Jill in Palo Alto, and I in London, Canada have put

my writing under a microscope to look at the fine tuning that has sometimes made meaning difficult. In reshaping it, allowing words more space, more time, more repetitions, we have heard new resonances. We hope you, our readers, will also.

Jill calls our creations "adaptations." I call them "moments." We do not call them poems. We both love poetry and we do not presume. We offer them with Sophia's proverbial grain of salt. Too much of her salt makes her wisdom bitter; just enough brings out the flavor.

A rose is a rose is a rose. By whatever name, we hope the images come home to your hearts in *Coming Home to Myself.*

2

Women's Lives, Women's Stories

Jill Mellick

A MUTUAL JOURNEY

This book *was conceived* one dawn as I was checking a quote from Marion I was including in a book. There it was: an inner voice declaring, "*Someone—sometime—should gather Marion's essential comments into one publication.*" Women who see me for psychotherapy tell me they often pick up Marion's books and open them anywhere, finding, "by chance," just what they need. I went on looking for the quote. Then I heard another, amused voice: "Well?" I couldn't believe my psyche was planting the seed for a new book before my current one was even published.

I leafed through *Addiction to Perfection*. Sentences and paragraphs containing strong images leaped out. I typed them out, each image to a page. When I looked at them, they demanded line breaks for better contemplation. The line breaks led to some restructuring of word flow. Quickly, the melody lines I had always heard in Marion's more orchestral prose began to sing a capella.

After I had played with these creations for days, I landed in reality with a spine-bruising thump. What was I *doing*? And who invited me? Yet the idea wouldn't leave. I found myself quoting lines when I was in session. People remembered them, often whispering them to themselves for days. I decided that, even if I were not the person for this project, it had merit. The next time Marion and I were together, I would show her these adaptations and suggest that *someone* might do something similar—preferably she, herself, or her husband, Ross, a poet and literary critic.

It seemed inevitable that Marion and I should have explored this idea as we walked through Whole Foods, an excellent food market in my home town of Palo Alto. As we wandered through its rich landscape—pyramids of bell peppers, towers of grains, hills of aromatic breads—we could barely remember what we had come to buy; our excitement about this wild idea was growing. The meeting of body and soul, which lies at the heart of Marion's life and work (and my own), was playing itself out in our simultaneously putting milk in the cart and imagining this book.

Surely this is what women do, how women walk through life, separately and together—never doing one task at a time, never moving in one realm at a time. Rarely is one activity segregated from another; rather each is woven into the complex fabric of daily responsibilities and relationship. The sacred and the heartfelt suffuse the ordinary.

Despite the comfort of putting bread and tea and irises into the cart, I found myself diffident about my possible role. Yet Marion responded with her usual blend of nonjudgment, openness, and discerning curiosity.

After lunch, I showed her the adaptations. What most pleased me was that she recognized her voice and essence in each. I invited her to read them aloud. They sounded like her to each of us. When they didn't, we both heard it and agreed quickly where and how to change it.

Marion refused to do the project herself and dubbed me "it." Her one reservation was my using the word "poetic" about her writing. She thought it sounded grandiose. She had never thought of her writing as "poetic." I disagreed but respected her reservation. I told her I would do the project only if she and Ross were to review each piece.

Over the next year, whenever we could carve out a few hours together, we would rework the latest pieces. Both having had previous lives as high school and college English teachers in Canada and Australia respectively, we found ourselves in happily familiar places—bandying word usage, punctuation, line breaks, puns, consonance, assonance, sustained metaphors, tense changes, alliteration. We trusted and respected each other's views and opinions in this realm, and our forthrightness had only mutuality in its tone. We became servants to the word and were united in that higher purpose. Later, Ross would run his ruthlessly honest, critical eye over each.

I am grateful to Marion for her generosity and for this opportunity to do so many things I love at one time. I am also grateful to Mary Jane Ryan of Conari Press who once again respected my ideas and idiosyncratic ways of realizing them. I am also thankful to Daryl Sharp of Inner City Books and Tami Simon of Sounds True Recordings, who each gave us free and unlimited rights to adapt material. Shambhala Press and Texas A and M University also allowed us free use of a generous amount of material. Dr. Jan Fisher worked with us on impeccable research, manuscript preparation, and cross referencing. My thanks to Stanton Mellick, Ph.D., Karen O'Connor, Ph.D., Paula Reeves, Ph.D., Jeanne Shutes, Ph.D., and Ross Woodman, Ph.D., who each supported aspects of my work in unique ways.

Working with Marion's prose in this way has been a delightful conjunction of passions and disciplines for me. Many of these we share: love of the English language and its literature, particularly poetry, both spoken and read; long histories as writers; long involvement with Jungian theory and practice; passion for essence; and profound and abiding respect for the healing power of metaphor.

Each of these pieces has been created from Marion's writing and talks. Criteria for selection are intuitive: the call of an image, the strength of a metaphor, the power of a tale or observation.

In the process, I felt more like an ocean swimmer than a writer. I delighted in being sustained by the larger oceanic flow of Marion's writing and then in feeling an image, a metaphor, swell like a wave, which I rode to shore until it reabsorbed itself into greater tidal directions.

If I caught the wave too late, I lost elevation and thrust from the metaphor; if I caught it too early, I wasted energy splashing around and was unprepared to cleanly ride the wave. If I abandoned the wave too early, I lost the benefit of being carried to clear shallows of consciousness; if I hung on too long, I beached my awareness where it could no longer move easily and all I could see was the metaphor being sucked back to sea.

Once the image came into focus, the form shaped itself, claiming its authority over me. I have added no ideas—to which the quickest scan of the original will attest. Rather, mine has been a quiet exercise in distilling essence. With Marion's encouragement, I have let explicatory material fall quietly away; then, with literary devices such as meter, repetition, and parallel construction, and by emphasizing through syntax relationships between images or thoughts, I have tried to reveal the armature, the shining bones of the writing.

When I reread narratives from Marion's personal life, quietly woven into the larger flow of her prose, I was startled. I was further startled when I reread sections that Marion flagged for me—stories and dreams she was now ready to identify as her own (Katherine's story in *The Owl Was a Baker's Daughter*, for example). As I lifted them from their explanatory and discursive contexts, their starkness stunned me. How did I miss their unflinching honesty before?

At first, I felt intrusive highlighting these stories as independent entities. My reaction seemed odd, given that they had been read or heard by thousands. I even felt odd showing them to Marion. I felt as though I had been reading her personal journals without permission. When we did sit down together to read these narratives—each with its umbilical cord to the book cut and tied—my experience was confirmed indirectly; Marion was silent and still, as though once more absorbing into heart and body her original experience.

Reviewing them quietly together, making small changes here and there, we spoke sporadically. I did mention how strongly working with these stories affected me, how I needed to work slowly with each until my heart could accommodate its impact. I said little else; the narratives were their own commentary.

Marion did ask one question, half to herself: "I wonder why people sentimentalize my writing. These stories aren't sweet, Jill."

I ventured a recent understanding. "You provide a gentler, larger context in which to hold more shocking material. You soften the impact. You make it easier for us to digest. Even when you talk, you balance a terrible story with humor. I'm not being as protective here. These stories: when they're removed from their context, they are stark, they are from the bone, they are shocking." I paused briefly. "Is this acceptable to you?"

Marion also waited a little. I could almost see her listening to her bones to hear whether they resonated with the bones of the narratives. Then she answered, "This is the way they are for me. This is what happened, Jill. No, I don't want to soften them. The Crone tells life as it is."

Many of the other stories belong to Marion's friends and to some who have been in Jungian analysis with her. There is no sentimentality here, just silent receptivity, nonjudgmental observation, and fierce, tender honesty. Marion also makes clear that while we might hold another's pain with a loving heart, we cannot remove it. Our souls must heal and grow in their own time. These stories remind us to receive nonjudgmentally both our own and others' unveiled moments of light and darkness. They remind us of the ways in which we each struggle with demons and dance with angels.

Marion is happiest when she knows that her writing has proven to be a helpful departure point for our own journeys, considerations, and insights, independent of hers. We encourage you to use this book in just that way.

I hope I have done my dear and respected friend's imagery justice by catching more waves than I have lost and by lightly riding their graceful, spiraling forms home, only to begin the journey again.

Growing Things in Darkness and in Light

Rare is the woman or man who arrives in adulthood unscathed by the vicissitudes of Western contemporary culture. Most of us have developed creative adaptations to make up for the fact that our movement, both inner and outer, is frequently impeded by old injuries that flare up.

These pages gently, fiercely bring us into the presence of some possible truths about the adaptations we have made as women. They invite us to be courageous enough to see—without collapsing—what we have fled from seeing in ourselves and others. As women seeking to grow into psychological and spiritual maturity, we need to acknowledge the subtle and not so subtle spiritual, cultural, emotional and physical damage we have experienced and to consciously choose new adaptations.

Healing does not mean wallowing in or identifying with injury. Nor does it mean defensive inaction. It means having the courage to see, acknowledge, grieve, and repair the holes ourselves (with, if we are fortunate, loving help from others). It means moving on, patches and all.

Marion alerts us to places of injury, to what we might have sacrificed in order to fit into a patriarchal culture. In capitulating to this unconscious patriarchal energy, we have been giving up even more than our souls. We have been handing over other birthrights: the right to our own feelings, and the right to take up conscious residence in our body—with love.

Often this self-betrayal, which happened silently and effortlessly in childhood, reemerges through the appearance of an addiction in later life. Marion makes many references to food addictions. These were the starting point of her work with the abandoned feminine and the need for its redemption. It quickly became clear to her that the suffering of addicts is not relevant to them alone. They are the canaries in the mine. Their cries are first. Their suffering alerts us to what is suffocating us in our dark and indentured daily descents into the perilous shafts of patriarchal society. Addictions are spiritual rituals that have been played out in a material world—accommodation to principles and rules, perfectionism, power, sexual longing and insecurity, pursuit of the perfect body, alcoholism, drugs, success in business, being the perfect mother (or all of these). Only through seeing these as metaphoric expressions of longing for soul and its rituals can we transcend limited lives and visions.

Ursula LeGuin, in a commencement speech given years ago to the women of Mills College in Oakland, California, emphasized that women grow things in darkness, not in light. It is darkness—with its secrets, earthiness, and joys, with its pains, losses, and despair—that we celebrate.

The woman who takes the time to grow herself in the darkness becomes familiar—perhaps for the first time—with the real source and containment of her psychic strength. No longer is her strength dissipated in obeying an idealized father figure, in pleasing a lover, in trying to satisfy a perpetually unsatisfied mother figure, in accommodating to a patriarchal organization or culture, in appeasing the inner witch who tells her she is worthless. No longer is her strength lost to obeying compulsions, drives, and obsessions that can slip in during the dark night of the soul and substitute for the real thing.

And what is the real thing, the thing for which she longs? The love affair with her own spirit, the inner marriage that commits her to her destiny, the rituals of soul that feed her deepest hunger, and the sense of being pregnant with her Self, her creative essence.

The journey to India that Marion describes in this book contains experiences that characterize all of our mythic journeys into the farthest regions of ourselves in search of the real thing: awakening; the call; the journey; the descent; the darkness; a healing crisis; an epiphany; the ascent; accepting unlikely companions on the journey; new visions of self and the world.

Later, Marion tells the story of an initiation on Krishna's birthday. Once again, we find the pattern characteristic of all initiations: the planning of the expected journey; the invitation to the unknown; the placing of trust in the situation and in one who initiates; the loss of the known and the entry into the unknown; the loss of personal identity; the fear of the initiation; facing the fear; active surrender; the epiphany; the restoration of personal identity; the return to the known world, this time with more spiritual understanding and lived knowledge; the long integration of the experience into daily life. These are developmental steps we all face if we actively surrender to the call of our soul.

To become whole, body and soul, we need to depart from the safety of the childhood house of beliefs into the wilderness, into the cave, with only the psychic necessities. We rarely have the safety of leaving one house of beliefs when we can clearly see the new house ahead lighted and warm. More often, we need to leave the old without any promise of the new, need to spend time as forest dwellers, just surviving. If we do survive, we find that we are no longer handmaidens to an outer authority that rules by principle rather than loving mutuality; we have reached a new cycle of maturity where we are consciously connected to our hearts, our bodies, our deepest values, and the people we love.

Our meandering paths into this new home are various, as these stories show. For each of us, there is a unique journey—it can come through the mind, through the body, through creativity, through the heart, through dealing with addictions, through age and cronehood, or through a unique mix of these.

We know that our journey to our old, new home is cyclical, that we shall never move in once and for all, and that we are well accompanied by other women and by ourselves. This book is also a companion on the journey, an encouragement, and, we hope, a source of quiet contemplation in which you might find your own rich images and creativity.

THE MEANDER PATTERN OF OUR LIVES AND STORIES

The feminine principle described in this book is neither linear nor unidirectional in its development. Catherine Bateson, in *Composing a Life*, remarks that women's outer lives are rarely led along trajectories toward unchanging goals. They are complex patterns of tasks, passions, and responsibilities that *intentionally live in response to* changing demands. To evaluate the achievements of such lives by objective linear measures is to miss the truth of how we really experience our lives and what we really value.

As women, we teach and pass on our wisdom through story—and we have done so through the ages. Story is one of the strongest containers for pain, joy, wisdom, fear. These stories in this book are no more linear than our lives. They don't begin, climax, and end where we might expect; they cycle back and forth through the maze, meander into the light, and disappear again into the dark.

This meander pattern—this map of the feminine spirit moving through women's inner and outer lives—informs the movement of Marion's original prose and these adapted contemplations. Through taking images important to you into body, heart, and soul, you can deepen the experience of your inner and outer journeys. Each journey has its gifts. Not all of the gifts are welcome but each does, indeed, carry the potential for quiet transformation.

WAYS TO DEEPEN YOUR WORK WITH THIS BOOK

Read with Your Body. Trinh Minh Ha, author of *Woman Native Other* reminds us that many women write not with the head but with the whole body. This kind of writing requires a different receptivity.

When you read this book daily, dip and surface, wander, alight. Do not bind yourself to reading word by word, line by line, page after page. As Marion says, if you miss the meaning the first time round, don't worry; it will pass by again in a new form. Read each piece more than once. The first time, read with your intuitive eye. The second, feel the body's resonance with phrases; these are the words that are plucking the strings of your heart and soul. When you reverberate, lay the book on your lap and go within. Actively open up to the image; experience the image taking up residence in your bones.

These are designed to be read daily, one at a time. But, if you are reading for longer periods, make time at least once an hour to get up and move. The body needs to allow the reading it is absorbing to move through it. Stretch, walk around the block, do deep breathing, move to music for five minutes—but do not sit for hours immersed in reading this book while your patient body waits in discomfort for you to return to it. That would contradict what you are reading!

This book does not ask to be read; it asks to be lived. To read with our whole body, we need more than a minute and a seat. No longer is it truly satisfying to snatch a moment between waking and sleeping, between throwing out the garbage and throwing on the pasta. Of course, if these moments are all we have, they are worthwhile. If they are all that we *ever* have, we miss experiencing the deep, abiding, embodied shift in consciousness. Open to a reflection at random. Become the quiet student of the intersection of randomness and meaning: trust the synchronicity of where the page opens for you each day. Work with one piece daily. Let your intuition and body be the authorities on how it is most fruitful for you to explore these. Quietly dance, paint, contemplate or otherwise embody these reflections.

Many of us say, when we reread journals from years

earlier, that we are shocked at how much we knew and have since forgotten, only to learn again in the next cycle of living and experience. "Why don't I remember the first time?" we ask, shocked, wondering why we spend so much energy on inner work that seems to vanish into the netherlands of our unconscious. We all know why, really: we continue to learn the same things again and again at each spiral in the path, each time taking the understanding deeper, each time embodying it more, each time able to recall it more quickly in demanding times. In a similar way, these pages might be able to remind you of what you already know deep down.

A Place of One's Own. When Virginia Woolf delivered her lecture on the importance of having a place of one's own, she spoke to Everywoman. If we are committed to tending our inner lives, we need a physical place in which to do this without interruption or intrusion. If you are reading this half-seated on a chair in the kitchen, munching, partly distracted by your need to prepare dinner, or your children's needs for a snack, you are probably missing any deep shifts in awareness you might experience.

Many women enter my consulting room feeling squeezed out of their lives—only to realize that, on a literal as well as metaphoric level, they have no place to call their own. However, even in a crowded home, simple changes can create a minimally private place. If you have not already done so, clear a space, no matter how small, that is yours alone. By your making this space physically, emotionally, and spiritually yours, it can become your temple.

In Japan, temple paths closed to the public often have a small, round stone tied four ways with string at the entry. A subtle, silent, effective gesture. If you live in a crowded space with house members who might not respect such a simple sign, you might even use a locked closet. Size doesn't matter (although it helps, undoubtedly!). What matters is your attending to your need for solitude. If even closet space is unavailable, make a temporary place for yourself. Lay out a special cloth or shawl on the floor. Place on it the things you want to use—paints, music. Keep a journal beside you for notes, drawings, mandalas, dreams—a large, cheap, blank book. This place and its tools will become treasured symbols of your time alone.

Create an Altar. When you have established your private place, you might consider adding a personal altar for certain kinds of inner work including the creative work this book is based on. A box can function as a movable (and closable) altar. Cover it with material whose color, history, or feel is quieting. Select symbols that will keep you mindful—of what you value, of who you are at your best, of how small you are in relation to larger forces at work in the universe. Choose pieces according to your spiritual or religious tradition. Preferably do not include any (or many) strongly connected with important people in your life. This time at your altar is for you alone. For example, your children might be central in your life and you might love parenting; however, this time and place are set aside to explore who you are *beyond* your daily roles.

Tend your place daily in a simple way consonant with your beliefs—a prayer, a meditation, a hymn, a chant, a quiet walk around the circumference, a vase of fragrant flowers, a sprig from a tree, a stick of incense, a candle. Do this with quiet attention. When you finish using your space, you might like to reverse whatever ritual you began with, covering private materials until the following day.

Choose Clothing Consciously. Be both practical and symbolic in your choice. Choose carefully what you wear for inner work. Choose it for comfort so that you can dance, paint, and read in it. Choose it, too, for personal significance. Do the color and fabric put you in touch more with your inner life? How have you used it in the past? Can you see yourself using it in this way now?

Play Music. Music creates an invisible yet palpable environment, and evokes a rich response from the body. Select favorite music to play during your reading or creative exploration: quiet music for meditation; flowing and smooth for movement; rhythmically varied for quick and slow gestures; and rousing for caged emotion. It may be wise to choose music you do not associate with a particular person or moment. Unless you intend to evoke new understanding of old memories carried in your body, choose music you will associate purely with your time alone.

Consider Using a Mirror. Our healing and growth comes from accepting ourselves for who we are, free of labels. At both real and symbolic levels, looking at ourselves in the mirror, being able to not only tolerate but celebrate looking at ourselves, can be helpful. If it feels timely and appropriate, use a large mirror for creative contemplation.

Explore Through the Arts and Dreams. Our soul speaks to us through metaphor and symbol and we best experience and express these through the creative arts. To explore your whole-body responses to these contemplations, you need little money and absolutely no talent. Newsprint and oil crayons or chalks are enough—plus a willingness to let your body make marks on a page. If you wish, keep malleable modeling clay on hand. For simple mask making, paper plates, poster paint, and cheap brushes suffice. Finger paints and finger paint paper also encourage full body expression.

Show others only creative pieces that you are really ready to have seen by other eyes. As Marion's image of the chrysalis reminds us, we need to protect what is gestating until is has been born and grown. This is delicate business, which gathers energy in the cooking pot of inner work. Lift the lid too soon or too often, and the food will never cook.

Metaphors, similes, symbols, and images abound on these pages. Find creative ways to express the effect certain images have on you—through collage, dance, claywork, haiku, poetry, personal story, or painting. Do not try to represent the image realistically; rather, focus on expressing the feeling you get from the image. Explore these images through movement. If you are working with a particular kind of body therapy, integrate your experience of these images into those times.

Record your dreams as you read this book and review recent dreams. Can you find threads of the themes that weave through these pages? How do these dream images play out in your life?

Exploring the inner world through creative expression is an important part of psychological healing and development. If you are unfamiliar with or want more ways to use simple media to enhance your inner life and dream work, *The Natural Artistry of Dreams* provides many easy ways for "nonartistic" (and artistic) people to explore the creative unconscious—through fairy tale and myth, poetry making, mask making, dialogue, movement, energy paintings, claywork, and ritual.

We read with more than our minds. So do not be too respectful of these printed pages. Mark them up! Mark lines to which your body responds with pleasure, tears, restlessness, stupor, anxiety. Note briefly on the page your body's response. Photocopy or transcribe pieces that carry intensity for you. Speak them out loud. Does a common theme weave through them? What is the smallest thing you can do this week to bring this new insight into your daily world?

List questions that come to you about yourself. Your questions are more valuable than the answers (which change from day to day). Don't bother to write in full-sentence, linear format. Jot down images, memory flashes, phrases. Intuitive insights are like fish in the water; they flash in the sunlight and then dive deep again, only enticed to the surface again by morsels of conscious attention.

Let the metaphors on these pages dance through your imagination. Allow the images to take up residence in consciousness, heart, and body. Once embraced, they will continue to grow in the chrysalis. One day, they will emerge, mature, as butterflies in your psychic life.

ABOUT THE PAINTINGS

The landscape paintings that divide each section carry a story. For years, several other women and I assisted at Marion's summer retreat for a small group of women. The five-day retreat was held on ShaSha, Marion and Ross's jewel of an island in Georgian Bay in Ontario. To reach the island was a pilgrimage just in itself; we left our lives behind and, as the boat made its way through the tricky channels between the islands—the journey prepared heart, soul, and body for the intensity of the days to come. In the same way, the voyage back allowed a gentle transition into our daily worlds.

To stay on the island brought healing and a beauty that haunts our dreams still. We listened to each others' stories, wept, laughed, sang, woke with the dawn, listened to loons, fought mosquitos, visited natural stone altars, lit candles, took turns cooking, braced the house against thunderstorms, and anointed our own and each others' bodies in the breathtakingly chill, clear waters of Georgian Bay. Over the years, I recorded that landscape in different media. I hope that these watercolors invite you into your own inner ShaSha, where you will spin, in spirit, one more thread of that invisible web that connects our community of women.

3

Learning to Trust & Receive

Infants *have central lessons* to learn after birth. As developmental theorists have described them, they need to learn to trust and receive from their caretaker, their environment, and ultimately themselves.

Because we are human, some of these lessons are incomplete. We might have learned—not inaccurately from the difficult situation into which we were born— that at least one of these three is not fully trustworthy. Such early learning dies hard. As adults, we have had years to confirm our findings. It takes leaps of faith for us to learn to trust and receive again.

As you reflect on trust and receptivity, consider the people you trust, in what areas you trust yourself, and what aspects of the environment you trust.

—J.M.

The fear of receiving resonates
in the deepest levels of the psyche.
To receive is
to let life happen,
to open to grief and loss,
to open to love and delight.

———

Only when we experience trust
in the mother's love—
through dreams or waking life—
can our body surrender its defenses.
Only then can it move
to a new sexuality
with woman or with man.

If I surrender
to what you're saying,
if I take a listening role
while you're talking,
I take in what you are saying.
I receive.
There is such energy in receiving.

––––––––

No amount of therapy
can heal a heart that cannot trust.
To learn to trust
is often
the heart of the therapy.

I use the word *mystery*,
rather than *magic*.

I loved magic.
Something magic was always going to happen.
When it did, it never did anything
but land me in trouble.

Mystery is the depth of the sacred.

The second daughter:
she was second, always second.
Her father rarely noticed her;
her mother, she always feared.

Only one thing she knew for sure:
what her mother was,
she was not.

She swung into life in red heels
and fell in love
with a handsome priest
who loved her
and who, of course,
had to give her up.

She came to know herself
through the gentle love
of a woman.

She was crying.
I don't know what to do
You tell me I have to recognize my feelings.
Most of the time I don't do anything
I want to do because I don't feel it would be right.
I was driving here,
and I had a desire—
to bring you a muffin.
I know you would love a muffin,
but no I won't buy it.
You don't take your analyst a muffin.
But then I got into such a state,
I was just sweating,
because I wanted to get the muffin so much.
I stopped the car, went back,
got the muffin,
and I have the muffin in the bag,
but I don't know whether to give it to you or not.
I feel like such a stupid child,
but I don't know what to do.
Well, I said, *I want to receive the muffin.*
I broke it in two.
And because she was received,
it was a communion.

So long as we're doing
one two three around the floor,
dancing is a bloody bore.
Only when we surrender
to the spirit of the music
can we truly dance.

———

Never interpret a work
until the work has had a chance
to interpret itself.

We receive life through our orifices:
eyes, ears, noses, pores, vagina.
When we truly receive,
we grow continually.

We are terrified of trust,
terrified of making ourselves vulnerable.
The leap into forgiveness is immense.
And after the leap, again the waiting.
And again another opening into love,
And again the terror.
It's the body that's terrified.

4

My Body

O*ur bodies,* with all their blessings and blemishes, give us pleasure and pain. They are also a vast, often untapped source of wisdom. Because most of us are in a culture that devalues the information our body gives us, we can fail to see, hear, taste, touch, and smell the subtle signals it sends us—in waking and sleeping—about our emotional states, spiritual well-being, physical health, and mental functioning.

You can begin to listen to those signals and to send constructive signals back to your body in many ways, using imagery, meditation, biofeedback, touch, and simple, loving attention.

Research and experience indicate that mind and body are not separate but part of a seamless, intricate network of intelligence. From a more intuitive perspective, your body can be considered a reservoir of cellular memory, wisdom, and guidance. If you attend, it can richly reward your journey into the unconscious with understanding about your deepest being and about the ways in which you might find healing and wholeness.

—J.M.

A body whose wisdom
has never been honored
does not easily trust.
An animal with a crazy trainer
    learns crazy habits,
runs wild.

———

When we take ourselves seriously,
we accept the responsibility
of knowing and loving our body.

Body work is soul work.
Imagination is the bridge
between body and soul.
To have healing power,
an image needs to be taken
into our body on our breath.
Only then can the image connect
with the life force.
Only then can things change.

The ego that refuses to submit
to the demands of the body
will eventually have to submit
to the powers of nature.

———

If the dream says something is wrong
with your body, check.
Long before you do, your body knows
when something is wrong.

If you can listen to the wisdom of your body,
love this flesh and bone,
dedicate yourself to its mystery,
you may one day
find yourself
smiling from your mirror.

How many people do you know
who are willing to trust
their deepest understanding?
Test body wisdom in your office:
just try asking your boss
to breathe a decision
into his belly to check its resonance....

Body work, like dream work, is soul work.
Body and dream illuminate
the point where spirit and matter
touch and do not touch.

Energy enters you
from the one sleeping beside you.
If that energy is depressed, angry,
doesn't like you tonight,
it might appear in your dreams.

————

If we breathe deeply,
feeling erupts,
grows too intense for us.
So we keep our breath shallow.
To breathe deeply
is to receive
and that is the feminine incarnate.

To be in my body
also means to suffer.

———

Often we listen to a cat
with more precision
than we listen to our body.

We cherish the cat.
It purrs.
Our body may have to release
a scream, a symptom,
to be heard by us at all.
Too often, our soul can find
no other way to be heard.

To sit in a chair and analyze
is heady stuff,
but it does not help you
live the power of the image.

Put your image into your body.
Does it waken a response?

Of course:
your rage, your grief,
your great Buddha laugh.

Just put the image into your body
and wait.

This is your body,
your greatest gift,
pregnant with wisdom you do not hear,
grief you thought was forgotten,
and joy you have never known.

Give your body an hour a day.
If it's not worth an hour a day,
there's nothing
your body can tell you
and not much
anyone else can do.

5

Beyond Addiction & Possession

Usually, *we associate* "addiction" with food, drugs, and sex. Yet anything that begins to dominate and control our lives, *regardless of cost to our well-being*, can become an addiction—perfectionism, work, order, analytic thinking, approval, money, the Internet, intensity, worry....

When addicted to an emotion, thought pattern, or action, we are powerless to resist or exercise choice; we engage in unconscious repetitions that seem to have meaning at the time, but later appear empty, without purpose. We are possessed again and again by a familiar yet alien drive that overrides all else. We become obsessed with obtaining, usually through an inner or outer ritual, something not tangibly obtainable such as peace, love, or wholeness.

If we can recognize the addiction or state of possession and understand what it is really trying to give us, we can patiently begin to provide for ourselves what we truly desire in less costly, longer-lasting, and more effective ways.

As you turn these pages, reflect on ways in which you might recognize and break free from obvious and subtler patterns of addiction and possession.

—J.M.

Illness or addiction can be the pathway to the feminine side of God.

———

What is my addiction trying to tell me?

A compulsive relationship
may be just the one we need
to work our way
into a conscious relationship.

―――――

If you find yourself
falling in love again
with the wrong man
and you can't help it,
take one minute
to shout in your own ear,
What am I doing?

The last curtain was the best.
The sets had been struck before we left.

We had a party—a memorable party.
The discipline over,
we clung to a world
that no longer existed.
We danced, ate, and drank
in no-man's land—
hadn't quite left,
hadn't quite returned.

About two in the morning
he crossed the room to thank me—
deliberate, serious.
But the party's not over, I said.
There's no performance tomorrow.

I have to go now, he said.
Quiet, decisive.
I have some serious drinking to do—
a rendezvous
with the one he had loved all his life
but could never marry.

I remember standing
in the midst of the dancers
looking into his proud eyes.

It was on my tongue to tell him
there was plenty of booze on the table.
But I sensed that was irrelevant.

Possession that drives us
can be our yearning
for conscious femininity.

———

Sexuality without love is matter without spirit.

She had been
an outstanding student,
a good athlete,
a good leader.

At twenty-three, she was eating
nothing but popcorn,
unable to make decisions,
unable to speak to others
for fear they would load her
with more work.

When she could work no longer,
she entered the hospital.

Weeks later,
she showed me her lists—
yearly, monthly, weekly,
daily, special—
each organized perfectly.
I can't help it, she said.
If one thing is missing,
what else might be?

Can you make room, I asked.
for spontaneity?

She dutifully agreed
and one week later showed me her daily list:
"2:15-2:30 P.M.: Spontaneity."

She is riding home on the subway.
She decides she won't alight
at her usual stop.
There's a muffin stand one stop earlier.
A walk would do her good.

She stays on.
She is nervous.
Two more stops,
she's out,
forgets the panic in the dark,
races back to buy them—
holy, hated, taboo muffins.

She is alone, of course.
She is already being walked.
She hurries home,
locks the door,
unplugs the phone,
puts on her always dress,
takes her always position,
and begins.

Loved, secure,
protected, enthroned,
at first she is calm.
The calm becomes ecstasy
and she becomes wolf.

If she is obese,
she falls into bed in a stupor.
If she is thin,
she puts her finger down her throat.

Possessed but not possessing,
she feels betrayed.
The goddess did not appear.

We view ourselves as works of art.
Somewhere in us there is
a perfect image,
a perfect work,
a well-wrought mask
that cuts us off
from flesh and blood.

Our real terror is that the work,
being precious,
may, in an instant, be destroyed.

Medusa wants everything
permanent, perfect,
engraved in stone.

———

We are all addicts.
We experience ourselves
as emptiness
swinging in empty space
between spirit and matter,
located nowhere.
Metaphor can heal.
Metaphor can link
spirit and matter.

6

Beyond Perfection & Duty

Having *high standards* and a sense of duty that transcends personal self-interest is laudable. However, when our standards are so high that we deem ourselves unacceptable unless we meet them, we are in trouble.

We know yet forget that to be human *is* to be flawed. Even the finest endeavor contains minor imperfections. In some Eastern cultures, certain works of art are deliberately flawed so that the gods will not be angry because an artist is competing with their perfection.

Perfectionism and blind duty can ravage a woman's body, spirit, emotions, relationships, self-respect, self-care, and equanimity. As a goal, perfection is usually lethal because it is never met and our failure leaves us with the pain of comparison. And doing one's duty is empty and soul-withering unless it is fed by love.

—J.M.

As long as we try to transcend ourselves,
reach for the sky,
pull away from ground and into spirit,
we are heroes carved in stone.
We stand atop the pillar alone
blind to the pigeon's droppings.

Do not try to transform yourself.
Move *into* yourself.
Move into your human unsuccess.
Perfection rapes the soul.

I was committed to becoming conscious
as quickly as possible.
Then suddenly, a black hole.
Chaos.
I knew the only solution
was to understand exactly
what was going on.
I read day and night for a week.

Bursting with knowledge,
I leapt into his office.
I knew what was wrong with me
and I knew how to cure it.
I spent the hour elaborating,
weaving profundities.
He wilted in his chair.
The more he wilted,
the faster I talked.
At the end of the hour,
he silently helped me on with my coat
and took me to the elevator.
With a twinkle in his eighty-year-old eyes
he pushed the button.
If I were you, Mrs. Woodman,
I would take my animus for a good drink.

I was so angry I didn't even take him a muffin.

If we are trying to live by ideals,
we are constantly plagued
by a sense of unreality.

———

It is easier to try
to be better
than you are
than to be
who you are.

Perfection does not allow for feeling.

———

Perfection is not interested
in staying in the body.
It wants to fly,
wants ideals,
wants beauty,
wants truth,
wants light,
and you sure don't get these here.

Perfection massacres the feminine.
Our culture pulses to the pressure of perfection.

————

To move toward perfection
is to move out of life
or never to enter.

She has foolproof recipes
for everything.
If strictly followed
(and to follow is to follow strictly),
they guarantee success.

Her real world is the world of things,
things that work efficiently.

She is impatient of error,
having no room for it;
there is no need for it.
Anyone learning under her jurisdiction
will be oriented from the start
to objects and goals,
clearly defined.

Her daughter knows herself as a thing,
thinks of herself as an object
designed for high efficiency.
She does not know
her mother's knowledge
is not wisdom,
is without human meaning,
is without personal love.

Her daughter has no standpoint
of her own.
There is no danger
of her opening
to her own weeping.
There is no danger
of her singing
her own song.

Eventually we have to face the fact
that we are not God.

7

Reclaiming My Own Energies

We often look elsewhere for what we have already; we project. We turn to others to give us a level of acceptance we can only give ourselves. We invest people, institutions, situations, and things with certain attributes that they might indeed have, yet which do not belong solely to them but to us as well. We attribute to others flaws we need to come to terms with in our own character; we credit others with fine qualities that we are unable to acknowledge in ourselves; we turn to institutions and leaders to give us answers, to rescue us from confusion and helplessness, to bring a level of meaning and order that can come only from within. Every time we reclaim some of our own energies, stop projecting onto others attributes of ourselves, we become more whole, more present.

—J.M.

The ghostly lover
does not remain in the shadows.

She:
>   The day I married,
>   I married not the man I loved
>   but the man my father chose.
>   As I walked down the aisle, I said to myself,
>   *I'm not enough for him,*
>   *not good enough,*
>   *not beautiful enough,*
>   *not smart enough.*
>
>   He said *Jump*!
>   I asked, *How high?*
>   Finally, I did not ask again.
>
>   Now everything's gone wrong.
>   It's my fault.
>   I should have been different.
>
>   My inner home is a prison.
>   I do get out, only to return.
>   I cannot forgive myself for a crime
>   I must have committed,
>   though I don't know what it is.
>   My heart is in white knots.
>   The voice I hear within

is disdainful, says I am worthless,
won't let me live.
When I hear it,
I have no sexuality
and fear it will never come back.

He:
    I always feel her fear,
    but she rarely puts it out.
    Except in other forms.

    If I say anything against her,
    she pulls a power trip.
    She argues like a phony lawyer.
    When she gets angry,
    I draw back, become a nice guy.
    She sees that and grows more violent.
    I listen, I give sympathy.
    The calmer I get,
    the wilder she becomes.
    The more I try to meet her demands,
    the stronger, more insistent they become.

    I go up the mountain of niceness,
    but by heaven I come down fast
    into the valley of rage.
    Once I'm there, there's no road out

that's not divorce or the knife.

I am son, father,
no longer lover,
probably never husband.

———

A mother who is identified with being mother
has to have children who will eat
what she gives them to eat
and do what she wants them to do.
They must remain children.

A mother who is only "Mother"
makes her children eat
what she gives them to eat.
When there's a full breast,
somebody has to drink.

8

Unmasking Myself

We *all have roles* we need to play and masks (the "faces") we need to wear. Many are vital and constructive: parent, partner, employee. However, roles and masks can be harmful if they conflict with our values, ethics, well-being, health, or real nature. They are also harmful when they become the only way we know how to feel confident or acceptable. And they are harmful if we identify completely with them.

Some masks fit us better than others; some no longer fit well; others never really fit at all. Sometimes, as children, we learned to play roles that became so necessary to our survival that they took the place of the person we really are. Now, as adult women, we only know that something is wrong because we have a pervasive weariness, depression, emptiness, or sense of unreality about us, despite success in our outer lives.

Are you familiar with the roles and masks you wear? Which are helpful? Which compromise you? Who lies beneath the masks? When and where does she reveal herself?

—J.M.

Hypocrisy, sentimentality, distraction,
are veils that hide reality.

———

I look in the mirror.
I see the lines.
I put on makeup.

A tired, painted face.
I've aged ten years in two.
I've never felt my age before.

I want me.
Just me.
I won't pretend.
I want to live before I die.

One day perhaps you shall look
beyond the mask
into your own mirror
at your own reality.

Are you appalled?
Are the terrified eyes
that look back at you
the eyes of your own child?

Sentimentality robs us of our feeling.
Sentimentality makes us pity
those who really feel.
Sentimentality looks down on life
being fully lived
and betrays relationship.
It is terrified of real feeling;
real feeling blasts away sentimentality.

———

There is no growth without real feeling.
Children not loved for who they are
do not learn how to love themselves.
Their growth is an exercise in pleasing others,
not in expanding through experience.
As adults, they must learn to nurture
their own lost child.

There's personal anger,
but underneath
there's often universal rage;
And when we are possessed,
God help the man
who's on the end of that.

Deep rage is not about the man;
Deep rage is this:

Nobody ever saw me.
Nobody ever heard me.
As long as I can remember,
I've had to perform.
When I tried to be myself,
I was told, *That's not what you think,
that's not what you ought to do.*
So, just like my mother and her mother,
I put on a false face.
My life became a lie.

That's deep rage.

We have lived our lives
behind a mask.
Sooner or later
—if we are lucky—
the mask will be smashed.

What a relief to be human
instead of the god or goddess
my parents imagined me to be
or I imagined them.

9

Finding My Own Voice

To *find my own voice* is to give truthful expression to how I experience myself and the world I live in. I might or might not be "right" by others' standards and measurements. But I can be truthful to my experience and to my way of expressing my experience. Such expression is unique to me and to this moment.

Sometimes, we silence our beliefs in the face of self-doubt, self-criticism, fear of judgment, or lack of confidence in our capacity to express ourselves in the way that we believe others will respect and understand. While forces in the environment certainly push against our finding our own voice, all too often the force that silences comes from within.

There are many ways of finding your voice, both alone and with others: keeping a journal; working with symbols and metaphors in dreams and in literature; exploring verbal and nonverbal ways of expression through the arts. Talent is of no help or consequence in this kind of self-expression. The "voice" you find will be yours, with all its beauty and flaws.

—J.M.

She dreamed a voice told her,
Go to the attic and find a black box.
Still dreaming, she found it
and slipped her hand in.
She gently lifted out a bird,
tiny, skeletal, starving.
Stricken, she wept
for this bird she had loved as a child
and then forgotten.
Her tears changed its body
into a radiant small boy who said,
I only wanted to sing my song.

Such a dream will change your life
—if you remember you once had a song to sing.

The more I talk
the more my inner voice is saying,
No, that's not it at all.

———

Who am I?
What are my values?
What are my needs?
Am I true to myself?
Do I betray myself?
What are my feelings?
Am I capable of love?
Am I true to my love?

Femininity is taking responsibility
for who I am,
not only what I do,
not how I seem to be,
not what I accomplish.
When all the doing is done,
I have to face myself
in my naked reality.

———

However veiled,
the feminine
is always naked.

The feminine finds its own voice
in the virgin:
the initiated feminine
who is who she is
because her values and emotions
are grounded in her musculature.

———

Only by discovering and loving the goddess
lost within our rejected body
can we hear our own authentic voice.

———

Without our body we cannot speak truthfully.
We may think we are speaking the truth,
but if we lie down
and somebody puts a hand
on our heart and belly,
we will cry.
There's truth in those tears.

A life truly lived
constantly burns away
veils of illusion,
opening our eyes
to our uniqueness.

A life truly lived
burns away
what is no longer relevant,
gradually reveals
our essence
until, at last,
we are strong enough
to stand in our naked truth.

A man may be shocked
when he sees you've really changed.
He thought you'd been
scribbling in your journal
—a sentimental, little Victorian girl
writing in your little book,
naive and uninitiated.
Suddenly, when you say,
Look, this is what I think,
he can't believe
what's coming out of your mouth.
Mother puts up with anything.
Mother is unconditional love.
When you say,
See me as I am,
you are no longer mother,
no longer his ideal woman.
You've changed.
He thought you'd been
scribbling in your journal.

If we are full of rage
we have to get it out of our body.
We have to express it—
to ourselves—
or it will take another form,
perhaps illness.

———

Anger is personal; rage, transpersonal.
We fear becoming angry
because we are terrified
of being possessed by rage.
So we skate.
In our dreams we skate or ski,
It takes ice and snow to skate and ski.
Feeling is frozen.
Rather than live in summer and spring,
we freeze.
No gentleness, no flow!
We feel nothing:
no anger, no rage.
No love.
The heart is closed.

Medusa appears, dark and devouring,
there to do battle.
When we wake to her
we cannot move.
She turns our creativity to stone.
Do not give up.
Keep telling her,
Your voice is not mine.
Do not give up.
Use all your courage.
Use all your strength.

———

Don't talk about *being true to myself*
until you are sure
to what voice you are being true.

It takes hard work to differentiate *our* inner voices,
and in crises,
there is no time to waste.
So spend an hour a day writing.
Separate real from unreal,
what stays from what goes.
Then leap beyond anything you ever imagined.

If you travel far enough,
one day you will recognize yourself
coming down the road to meet you.
And you will say
YES.

10

Leaving My Father's House

Blind *patriarchal authority* as it shows itself in men and women, adheres to prevailing opinion and expectation, to standing rules and regulations. It values goals and achievement; linear thinking, rationality, observable phenomena, measurable outcomes, and right and wrong.

To leave our father's house is not to wage war against our personal fathers. It is an invitation to trust inner wisdom, an invitation that may ask us to stand up to unthinking, rule-bound authorities. It also invites us to confront those same forces *within.*

Finding our inner wisdom can be difficult. How do we find something if we neither recognize nor trust it easily, if we do not know we ever possessed or lost it?

We should not follow every urging, impulse, and intuition regardless of sound outer wisdom and information. We need discernment. But we can give our deepest values and perceptions at least an equal hearing. As you turn these pages, reflect on ways you can listen to inner wisdom and values in the face of forceful inner and outer rulemakers.

—J.M.

We discuss the feminine principle,
read our notes, talk fast,
our bodies wound in knots.
We contradict what comes out of our mouths,
use feminine language
to mask our patriarchal thoughts.

———

How does it feel
in your empty apartment,
hearing voices inside
you thought were outside?
Do you wonder if finding yourself
is all it's cracked up to be?
Can you be the person
you have always denied?

How does it feel
to leave your father's house?
Your father-husband's house?

How does it feel
to look in his eyes
and see yourself as betrayer
of the one man
who has always trusted you?

How does it feel
to leave the security of his love
even though he never knew
who you were?

In psychic incest, lines between parent and child
are unclear, weak, or nonexistent.
The daughter merges with the father,
both human and divine.

———

Matriarchs are often more authoritarian
than patriarchal men.

The message is the same:
In our dreams, we are trapped—
in our home,
in a tomb,
in frozen water,
in a sinking ship,
in the stillness,
in the darkness,
in a prison,
in a concentration camp,
in a cave with a rock for a door.

Old Mother God, Old Father God—
they keep us trapped.
And we do give up.
We pull the covers over our head,
and go back to sleep.

Only to dream of old dragons,
old alligators, old crocodiles
drinking our blood.
To dream of cold-eyed lawmakers saying,
This is the way it's always been done.
It works.
It will stay this way.
And you will obey.

Only to dream we are riding
in our father's old car,
and he is driving.
To dream
we are in our mother's kitchen,
eating food she is cooking,
not cooking our own.

— I'm cooking for her

Only to dream we are looking
through father's or mother's,
or somebody's, anyone's glasses,
but not our own.

Only to dream
a banquet is spread
and we cannot eat.

She lived to please him,
lover, jailer, father,
lived to share his pursuits,
to meet his standards of perfection.
She was his beloved
(her mother, absent or rival).

Now, in the night,
she dreams of her demon lover.
In the day, she enacts her dream,
fearing its power:
she loves a man who cannot marry
—too young, too old,
blond priest,
blue-eyed homosexual.
All through her life,
she arrives too late.
She lives without her body.

She dreams she is in a glass coffin.
From her prison, details have beauty.
In her aloneness, she imagines emotions.

Her husband is the perfect bridegroom,
the trickster, the small boy looking for mother.
She is goddess and mirror,
siren and friend,
femme fatale and sacrificing wife.

He is attracted to her girlhood purity,
her desire to sacrifice, to serve.
At first he may be flattered:
she sees him as a god.

Ultimately, he will reject her
knowing he cannot live
up to her demands.

If he matures, he will grow bored with her
whom he can never reach,
as she walks her tightrope above the abyss
and wonders why men call her cruel.

When he calls your feminine approach
rambling, lacking in clarity,
coherence, emphasis,
do you wonder if you are stupid?

How does it feel
to say *no* to the one man
to whom you have always said *yes?*

How does it feel
when you stand up to him
and reject all he has never questioned?

11

Active Surrender

In defeat, we are forced to lay down our sword; in active surrender, we consciously choose to lay it down. We consciously accept that certain things are beyond our control. We consciously accept that certain things should be beyond our control. We learn to separate out what needs action from what requires our acceptance and embrace. We choose the unknown.

Practicing active surrender is important because it is as much a source of energy and freedom as taking action is. And it is often needed when we approach situations with love rather than power.

—J.M.

Do you think I have a father complex?
I asked my analyst,
with just enough bravado
to cover my shame.
That is your destiny, he said.
Celebrate it.
You're going to walk that path
whether you like it or not.
You can go like a squealing pig
to slaughter,
or you can walk
with as much dignity as you can muster.

We are so sure
that to be receptive
is to surrender control;
that to open to fate is
to plummet through the dark.
We know no loving arms will open
to receive us as we fall.
We know we dare not;
the consequences would be fatal.

The door of our cage stands open.
We dare not walk through.
If we act out of instinct,
voice our feelings,
we open ourselves to fate.
Better, silence.
Better, the roles—
daughter, wife, mother—
as we have always—even half-heartedly—
understood them.

Indeed, we may be making
the only choice we can.

I dream I am
walking in darkness.
I come upon
a volcano, round and black.
I am not sure it is dead
or what I might stir up
if I jump in.
The mud is heavy, foul.

Then comes a voice,
more plea than command,
Throw yourself into the abyss.
I walk to the brink.
All around, the voices echo,
Trust.

I jump.
As I fall I see,
at the bottom of the abyss,
two golden S's,
Spiritus Sanctus,
float and unite to make infinity.
I land in its center
and infinity stands on end.
Its crown bursts into flame and carries me
to the top of darkness.

Just when the sun came to noon,
total eclipse.
Words must be spoken
but there is nobody to speak.
No body.

Where to go?
Down what street that does not
smell of dead lilacs?

He is gone.
Three words.
I open my mouth:
an animal howl.

———————

Fear keeps us chattering,
fear that wells up from the past,
fear of repercussions,
fear of blurting out
what we really fear.

Healing needs listening
with the inner ear,
stopping the incessant blather,
listening.

I was traveling alone;
this city, my last stop.
Fasting was part of my plan
to overcome the pain.
Six weeks of near starvation
had made me bodiless,
more ready to free myself into death
at twenty-five
than into life again.

I was crossing
from one railway station to another
when he forced me into the alley.
He said he would rape and kill me.

I tried to run. He was stronger.
I saw the man, I saw myself,
and accepted death.
He could not kill what had already died.
I relaxed and looked into his eyes.

His fingers loosened their grip on my throat.
You don't even fight,
you're no fun to kill.

If I'm going to die, I'm going to die,
I said quietly, never taking my eye from his.

He was confused.
I put my hands over his
and gently took them from my throat.
He began to cry, grabbed my wrist,
yanked me into a nearby pub,
and told me he had watched me in the train.
I had been unaware of him.
He believed
I was pretending to read,
was casting a spell,
was luring him into my web.
I listened and waited
and when he went into the urinal,
I escaped.

I returned home unraped,
ravaged, for the first time seeing
in his desperate eyes my stillness.

The house of cards collapses.
Somewhere, we think,
there must be joy.
It can't be all
must and ought and have to.
When the crunch comes,
we have to realize the truth:
we weren't there.

———

To surrender is to accept
life as it is:
winter today, spring tomorrow;
cruelty with beauty;
aloneness after love.

In fateful crises, we may really have no choice.

———

We know what we feel,
know what we desire,
then slowly surrender
to accept what is, and forgive.
What might have been
the salt of bitterness
becomes the salt of wisdom.
Sophia understands well
the salt that gives life savor.

When the path is blocked,
we can accept or fight.
When we fight, doors slam.
When we surrender to the mystery
and say,
Well, what do you need?
doors open.

———

Life becomes hectic.
We try to exert control,
create secure little pigeonholes,
believe we are in control.
And all the time we know
chaos leaps eternally
at our edges.

Whether we understand it or not,
sometimes we know
that Someone is moving us.
To know this
is to be known.

12

The Black Madonna: Embodied Feminine

In many cultures, important transcendent qualities are personified as divine beings. Some qualities are perceived as specifically feminine, and are widely represented by female deities. Certain central feminine qualities are personified in the figure of the Black Madonna.

She manifests in sexuality, in childbirth, in nature—in the earthiest sides of our womanhood. She is the mother of a divine son who embodies a new consciousness in the darkness that holds the light.

—J.M.

The Black Madonna is sacredness in matter,
the intersection of sexuality and spirituality.

———

The Black Madonna's energy has smoldered.
Rejected by the patriarchy,
now she is erupting
in the world and in us,
demanding conscious recognition.

The Black Madonna walked into the kitchen,
munched carrots, and said,
So where are your pearls?
The dreamer replied, *They're upstairs.*

Get them, she said.
The dreamer climbed the stairs.
The pearls were not there.
Shame-faced, the dreamer went downstairs.

Of course you couldn't find them, she said.
I found them—in a ditch.
You weren't taking care of them.
It's the third time I've found them.
I won't bring them back again.
Next time it's up to you.

The Black Madonna weeps at times.
At times she is austere.
At times her fierce humor
cuts through our daily madness.

———

The Black Madonna is larger than life itself.
Nature impregnated by spirit,
she presides over fertility, sexuality, childbirth.
She accepts her body as chalice for spirit,
presides over the sacredness of matter,
the meeting of sex and spirit.
Rejected by the patriarchy,
her energy has smoldered for generations.
Now she erupts in us and in the world,
demands conscious recognition,
demands redemption of matter.

When she comes in a dream,
She may take us on her lap,
put our head beside her heart,
and rock.

And we know
we have never heard that heartbeat,
never felt so loved.

Sometimes she is strict.
Her discipline is part of her love.
She knows what she is fighting.

13

Sophia: Feminine Wisdom

I f the sum total of our spirituality is larger than our minds can encompass, then we can better appreciate particular qualities through their personification as certain spiritual figures. The figure of Sophia carries, within certain Christian traditions, that aspect of our spirituality thought of as feminine wisdom. Her wisdom is rooted in experience, in compassion. She thinks with her heart and is more concerned with the processes than with the products of a life lived fully. She does not value the presence of power but the power of presence. We all carry Sophia in our hearts and when we connect to our feminine wisdom, we embody her in all her magnificence.

—J.M.

On Friday I sent the clothes
I would wear for my Sunday speech
to the hotel cleaners.
On Saturday night, at five, I called.
They said they'd been delivered
—*to a room.*
(They had no idea which.)
I would receive them—*sometime.*

They did turn up.
And I rose early Sunday to meditate
and work on my speech, then thought,
I'll put on those clothes
and see if they still fit.
The hem of the skirt was ripped out.
I'm not adept with a needle and thread
and have no idea how to hem
so you can't see the hem on the other side.
And I couldn't thread the needle,
(The thread was too thick for the eye of the needle.
If you've tried a hotel needle, you'll understand.)
My husband was still sleeping
so there I was, on the toilet, mending
and digging the needle into my finger,
and bleeding instead of meditating.

And I could hear Sophia laughing.

So if you dream of Isis—fine.
If you dream of your grandmother
—great mother—
and she becomes Her—
fine.
Call her Sophie,
Call her Anna.
Call her Buffalo Woman.
It doesn't matter.
Call her whatever
you like.

But call her.

If it bothers you, change it.
Try not to get stuck on little things.
God, Goddess;
Shiva, Shakti;
Yin with Yang
embracing Yang with Yin;
we get caught in old words.
Call it what you want.

But call it.

Sophia dances in the flames.
Horror and beauty blaze in her love.

———

To surrender to Sophia
takes strength and long travail.
She is opposition
transformed into paradox.

Sophia is
the receptive Being in whom
divine and human meet.

———

Sophia is the bridge.
She is the mystery.

———

Sophia is the stillness
at the center of the whirlpool,
the eye of the hurricane.
Without her,
there is no dance.

Sophia is the wisdom
that grows within each cell.
Beauty and horror
both blaze in her love,
and She is dancing in the flames.

———

Sophia wants things
moving,
breathing,
touching,
creating.

Sophia is
body opening to spirit,
illumination rising
from icy waters.

14

The Crone

If the *Black Madonna* may be said to carry our embodied spirituality and Sophia, to carry a timeless wisdom of the heart, then the Crone may be said to personify the wise older woman who has lived long, suffered loss and pain, survived to tell the truth to herself (and others if they are ready to hear), laughed with kindness at herself, learned to let go of expectations, and forgiven herself and others for their shortcomings. As you turn these pages, you might like to remember those women who have given you a glimpse of their hard-earned, lightly-held wisdom. Perhaps you will even want to find ways to express your appreciation to them inwardly or outwardly. In doing this, you might remember the wisdom of the Crone that is already taking up silent residence in your bones.

—J.M.

Age does not make a crone.
The fortunes and misfortunes of her life
do have something to do
with her maturing.

———

The Crone acts as a tuning fork
in an environment.
Because she is true
to her own feeling,
she rings a true tone
that resonates with others.

The Crone can afford to be honest.
She's not playing games anymore.
She brings you into that place
where outer conflicts dissolve
and you can experience your essence.

———

The Crone cuts.
She cuts with love.
Her sword has
a well-honed golden blade
and a silver handle.

The Crone has gone
through one crossroads after another.
She has reached a place of surrender
where her personal demands are no longer relevant.
She is a surrendered instrument
and therefore detached.

———

The Crone has nothing to lose.
She can be who she is,
can live with the naked truth.

The Crone has nothing to lose.
There is no power operating.
She has no reason to persuade you
to do anything
or to be anything
other than what you are.
She's a perfect mirror.

———

The Crone has seen enough
to be able to separate
irrelevance from essence.
She has neither time nor energy
to waste on superficialities.

The Crone is strong enough
to hold the container
in which men can experience
their hidden rage
without destroying themselves or others.
The Crone takes life
with Sophia's proverbial grain of salt.
She can smile at the divine comedy.

———

If the Crone hasn't lived
through her own crossroads,
don't trust her.
She'll want power.

To the Crone, detachment is not indifference.
It means she has lived,
and suffered,
and, having suffered,
can draw back
and see with her heart.

15

Conscious Femininity

Conscious *femininity* is not about being self-consciously female. It is an inner experience for both women and men. Yet, at a recent meeting of women—all committed to conscious femininity—when one woman asked, "What *is* it?" there was silence! We could not define it! Hours later it still defied definition, although the room resounded with stories and rich descriptions.

In these pages, we glimpse it in experiences of presence, process, paradox, embodied soul, thinking with the heart, receptivity, and resonance.

—J.M.

Feminine consciousness
is the transformative energy
that can contain the energies of matter
and, through the fire of love,
connect them to the energies of soul.

———

In man or in woman,
the virgin
has the courage to BE
and the flexibility
to be always becoming.

Lunar consciousness unites,
thinks with the heart,
incorporates past, present, and future
in time out of time.

———

The feminine
is an ocean of eternal being;
she contains the primordial animals,
contains the seeds for life.

The feminine is grounded
in the instincts;
she knows the laws of nature
and exacts them with ruthless justice.

———

The feminine
has slower rhythms,
meanders,
moves in spirals,
turns back on herself,
finds what is meaningful to her,
and plays.

The feminine
is always on the side of life.
loves life.
Loves.
If penetrated by the creative,
she flows into life
with a constant flow:
new hope,
new faith,
new dimensions of love.

———

The feminine is often lost to us
yet never forgotten in our dreams:
purses are lost;
a wild wolf bites our hand;
little cats die.

We must not only hear
the feminine,
but act.
If we abandon her,
she turns her dark face,
revengeful, depressed, suicidal.
We need to accept
that our lives
are turning inside out.

16

Integrating Masculine Energy

Qualities of active receptivity, resonance, loving presence, process, paradox, and intuition have been traditionally associated by many theorists with the feminine aspects of spirituality. Their complements have been traditionally associated by many with masculine aspects of spirituality including initiative, directedness, discernment, analysis, decisiveness, strength of purpose, and clarity of mind. Some women—particularly younger—might not find that these distinctions parallel their experience. However, most of us might agree that, for every characteristic that has been nurtured in us by culture and family, there is a complementary quality that has probably been nurtured less.

To be well rounded individuals, we need to find graceful ways to move back and forth between "feminine" and "masculine" qualities, ways that allow those opposites to act synergistically.

—J.M.

At the moment of awakening,
we have to ask real questions
and be prepared to take real action.
It doesn't matter any more
what mother did to me,
what father did to me.
Shall I stay in this job?
Shall I stay in this relationship?
Am I going to live,
even if I don't know what that means?

Solar consciousness
cuts and clarifies,
makes well-defined boundaries.

———

We must first awaken
to our needs, feelings and values.
Then the masculine can grow up
and say:
I shall stand up
for these needs, these feelings, these values.
I shall put them out there in the world,
I shall work with you in all your creativity.

Positive masculine energy
is goal oriented,
has the strength of purpose
to move toward that goal.
It disciplines itself
to make the most of its gifts,
physical, intellectual, spiritual.
It attempts to bring them into harmony.
It learns to hold the tension
between a firm standpoint and a surrender
to the creative feminine within.

———

Solar consciousness
analyzes and discriminates.

I am no sailor
but I love to crew:
he and I, barefoot and flying,
skim, toss, veer
with treacherous current and vagaries of wind
through the waters of Georgian Bay.

Poised, excited, he takes easy command,
straining to keep the craft upright—
strong body, keen mind in harmony,
tuned to the fierce energies
through which we sail.

One slip, one moment of indecision
would hurl us headlong.
We strain back over the water,
hang on with our toes.

We moor,
I step out, feet bloody,
thighs burning.
He takes down the sails,
ties the ropes, smiles,
and walks up the cliff,
confident, relaxed, erect.
He trusts his animal body.
The eternal has blown through.

17

The Inner Marriage

I t's easy to feel that we are only whole when we are in relationship with another person whose qualities complete our picture of ourselves, both inner and outer. We rely on or long for that person who, we believe, can give us a completeness, purpose, and meaning we think we cannot have otherwise. When we fall prey to this belief, we underestimate ourselves and overburden our loved ones with unrealistic expectations.

When we stop expecting another to give us wholeness, we can take the risk of finding our own sense of wholeness; we can discover and encourage our own complementary energies, the inner masculine and feminine aspects of ourselves.

—J.M.

Masculinity is in men and women.
Femininity is in women and men.
Develop each to its fullest.

In relationship, each needs
full masculine and full feminine
to make things flow.
We are still so far from that.

———

The first time we fall helplessly in love,
we are in love with our own projected image.
Slowly, after many projections,
we recognize they are all alike at their core,
these ones to whom we are fatally drawn.
Slowly we recognize ourselves.
We have been falling in love with ourselves.

The graveyard was just behind
the family homestead;
The movement from life to immortality,
merely an adjustment of focus;
immortality, a presence.

Her father presided
with puritan severity,
broken, at times,
by tenderness and warmth.
She lived to please him,
share his pursuits,
meet his standards of perfection.

Another entered her life
when she was thirty-one.
He was married.
How well she knew him, we do not know.
Three years later, he moved away.

Left her
with willpower and a mask
to cover the blistering wound.

She was the perfect seedbed
for the demon lover.
Every encounter with friend and flower
released bolts of energy.

Determined to save her life,
she wore only white,
tended her garden
and a few close friends,
baked daily bread.

And, in one year alone,
wrote 366 poems.

He isn't a god after all.
The real god is inside.
Slowly, you recognize
the illusions, the delusions,
the pain of human limitation.
Then gradually it dawns
what a huge mistake you've made.

Hold your divinity within.
Then ask yourself,

Do I love this human being?
You may find that you do;
that there's something noble in his suffering,
something noble in your own;
that you're walking parallel paths,
not holding each other up.

It's a marvelous thing,
to love another human being this way.

If we are depending on our partner
to make us whole,
we're in trouble.
Sooner or later, we shall feel betrayed.
Sooner or later, we shall hate the dependence,
Sooner or later, we may be the one
who does the betraying.
Wholeness is within.

Something, someone, more intense,
is luring her out of life.
Her ghostly lover was merely the altar boy
for this, her Demon Lover.

Fiery, suave, seductive with royal charm,
he lives at her core,
a lover-killer within.
His magnetism lures her
toward death.

Her God is sadistic:
does not say Yes to her prayers.
God is her demon assailant
and she, enraged.

Her heart could stop,
not from death
but from fury
at the inevitability of loss.

Her awareness of immanence
may yet turn her round
with will
to live her own life.

She can make a choice.
She can choose surrender;

demon can become daimon,
her spirit guide within.

His wounding may become his blessing
and he, her inner king,
her creative genius;
this union, the true creative act.

She need not succumb,
need not retreat,
nor need she harden into bitterness.
She can begin a love affair
with her own life.

Spiritual birth, like biological birth,
requires a union of opposites,
from which the sacred child is born.

18

Creativity

S*ome people think of creativity* as something that artists possess. It might be more helpful to think of it as Jung did, as an instinct. We can bring creativity to almost every life activity. Moreover, we can use certain imaginative forms of creative expression through the arts to explore personal, spiritual, and psychological development. These forms do not need artistic talent but simply artistic expression for the soul's sake. Metaphor, imagination, symbol can be said to be the soul's native language.

As you turn these pages, you might invite yourself to remember the ways in which you already express your creativity and quietly vow to yourself that you will also find other ways to free the creativity you ignore.

—J.M.

Creativity is divine:
the virgin soul opens to spirit
and conceives the divine child.
We cannot live without it.
It is the meaning of life,
this creative fire.

———

When *doing* is all we know,
being is just another word
for ceasing to exist.
When *being* begins to flow
through dance and paint and song,
joy is no longer luxury
but absolute need.

If you paint,
I say *yes, yes* to that.

If you use clay,
I say *yes, yes* to that.

If you set your dreams to music,
I say *yes, yes* to that.

I say *yes* to anything
that says *yes* to the soul.

In her dream
a pen, a paintbrush.

Do you ever paint?
> *Nope. No, I can't paint.*
> *My sister's a good painter.*
> *I could never paint.*

Her dreams are full
of brushes, colors,
a woman painting.

> *Something happened.*
> *I stopped.*

Her dreams are full
of brushes, colors,
a woman painting.

> *I really do love painting.*

Sooner or later
we have to take responsibility
for who we were born to be.

In our creating, we are created.

———

Just give him the paints.
Let him go to it
and discover his own soul.

If we give ourselves half an hour a day
with our creativity,
our dreams, our music,
the soul becomes quiet.
We are in our body
and we feel nourished.

———

Let your body become the music.
Let her sing.
Let your pen walk in the twilight
between consciousness and unconscious.
There, it will find
such images, such ideas
as you could never find.

Once you dance for a year,
it's part of your day.
I mean, it's prayer.
Dance your dreams each morning,
Let your images move in your body.

19

Dream Wisdom

Messengers *between* the creative unconscious and consciousness, dreams speak their own language, a language of image, symbol, and metaphor. When we bring our imagination, openness, and discernment to them, they are possible sources of inner guidance, wisdom, revelation, healing, and development.

Dreams live in a universe free of time and space restrictions. Only the fluidity of the arts—movement, poetry, myth, and art—truly carry their messages well to waking awareness. If we limit the dream to verbal analysis and reductive definitions, the dream dries up. However, if we feed our dreams with our creativity and curiosity, they will nourish our understanding for days, even years.

Let your memory bring you gifts from your dream world.

—J.M.

The dream keeps us
in touch with that soul
in which we all live.
The dream keeps us
in touch with our place
in that one creation.
The dream puts us
into a time and space
in which we are restored.

———

Our dreams give us the images
for our personal lives and for the earth.
Integrating these images
takes hours in meditation
and we may make fools of ourselves
when we first put them into life.
But when we've seen with new eyes,
when we've heard with new ears,
we can't go back.
However painful the fire,
we're in our own fire now.
We're learning what love is.

Our dreams disturb in order to illumine.

————

To make prose sense of a dream
subjects the dream
to a grammatical logic
that may be alien
to the symbolic logic
of the dreaming state.
The dream is closer
to poetry than prose.

We never know exactly
what a symbol means.
The symbol carries
meaning for the mind,
meaning for the heart,
meaning for the imagination.
We can never say,
That is what the dream means.
Years later we say,
Ah! That's what the dream was about!
A symbol opens and opens and opens.

————

If the dream uses a symbol
and you say, *That's bizarre!* Chuck it,
you're chucking gold.

Our banquet of dreams is spread each night.
We can choose to eat.
We can choose not to eat.

———

Write dreams down.
Work with them.
Talk with trusted others.
It will amaze you
how much comes through.
Be subjective and objective
at the same time.
Listen to your dream
with your third ear.

A dream can often tell us
what and where a problem is
long before a doctor can diagnose.

———

The dream arises from the instinctual world.

It usually comes after working on the body.
The dream will bring it to you:
a shift in sexuality,
a wave of creativity,
a welcoming of shadow.

———

God is the dream maker
revealed through the dream.

Dreams are the quickest way
into our inner world.
They astonish us with their wisdom
about past, present, future.

———

Once we know what the dream world is,
to be without it is to be rudderless.
The dream continually corrects
our waking course.

Sleep brings body into balance;
dream brings psyche into balance.

———

The dream's language is not two-dimensional.
It carries its meaning
through imagination, emotion, and intellect.

We say, *That's it! That's it. I've got it!*
We know who we are.
Then, feeling whole, we walk out the door
and run into a reality we barely understand.
Yet, still reverberating with that moment of
wholeness, we can say,
This, this is my inner truth.
I shall try to stand in that today.

Tonight may bring a new image.

We cannot take in the dream
when we have it.

We glimpse ourselves and think,
That's crazy! Can't be!
Will never happen!

One day we shall find ourselves
walking into an image from a dream
we had years ago.

———

If you don't believe
something is trying to bring you
to full potential,
the dream world is impossible.
It takes you through dark water,
demonic territory.
You'll say, *No more of this!*

Balance of wind and water.
A small sail boat
accommodating the wind:
that is the dream process.
It must follow the currents,
yet we must hold firm
on the rudder and the sail.

———

The dream comes
from the world of the eternal,
the great *I am*.

20

Holding Conflict Creatively

Holding *an inner* or outer conflict quietly instead of attempting to resolve it quickly is a difficult idea to entertain. It is even more challenging to experience! However, as Carl Jung believed, if we held the tension between the two opposing forces, there would emerge a third way, which would unite and transcend the two. Indeed, he believed that this transcendent force was crucial to individuation. A woman might be torn between leaving her husband for a lover and staying with him out of loyalty and guilt. If she can be quiet enough and step back from her conflict, she may find, to her surprise, that she now *wants* to stay with her husband because she feels a new kind of love for him, or she might find, again to her surprise, that what she really wants is to live *alone*. Or she may find new life in her lover.

Whatever the third way is, it usually comes as a surprise, because it has not penetrated our defenses until now. A hasty move to resolve tension can abort growth of the new. If we can hold conflict in psychic utero long enough, we can give birth to something new in ourselves.

—J.M.

Both arms on the cross,
we dare not drop the tension.

If we reject one part,
we give up our past;
if we reject the other,
we give up our future.

Whether we like it or not,
we need to hold to our roots
and build from there.

If we can hold the conflict of opposites—
what we want and
what destiny has ordained—
if we can hold
while mind thinks and heart feels
we can learn to think with the heart.

———

In our dreams, we dance
along a fence,
up stairs, down stairs,
on sands beside the sea,
on dance floors we have known
and on others we have yearned to know.
In dreams and in life, we dance,
holding our balance between the opposites.

I'm brave.
Brave also means
being nervous.

————

We are not animals only.
We are not gods only.

Sentimentality refuses to suffer,
fears the heat
of passion, anger, grief.
Real feeling is tempered in fire,
moves into conflict
and holds the opposites
until the new is born.

———

A free woman has a strong neck,
an open connection between heart and head,
a balance between reality and ideals.

So long as we divide ourselves
with ancient dualities—
spirit or matter,
white or black,
we cannot know
the sacredness of matter.
We are blind to the unity
that nurtures diversity.

———

Life is a continual attempt
to balance yin and yang.
The further we move toward radiance,
the blacker the energy that gathers
behind our back.
The more we force ourselves
to perfect our ideal image of ourselves,
the more overflowing toilet bowls
we shall have in our dreams.

What do we do
when everything rational says,
Let go!
and everything emotional says,
I cannot!

————

We can swing back and forth
between opposites indefinitely.
Better to stand
on the stillpoint
at the center.

21

Finding Meaning in Darkness

Certain things grow in darkness—babies, dreams, roots. . . . We often associate darkness with negativity, but darkness has both positive and negative sides. Dark times in our life might or might not contain inherent meaning; our view of this depends on our religious and spiritual perspectives.

Yet there seems little doubt that dark times can provide opportunities for the student of the heart to learn. Even times that seem ravaged by loss and pain can be used as occasions for us to grow and mature. By approaching situations from the point of view of the student, we might learn from the dark.

—J.M.

There's another way
to look at darkness.

———

Creative work comes from that level
where we share our suffering,
just the sheer suffering
of being human.
That's where real love is.

No matter how awful it is,
the truth sets us free.

———

Suffering and conflict
are one way to grow.
As life moves from phase to phase,
we suffer the death of one,
the birth of the other.

There is great danger
in trying to make everything sacred.

———

I almost envy them, sometimes,
the happy ones.
I'm sure they don't envy me.
They say,
You're always grief-stricken,
always worrying,
always trying to understand,
always trying to 'bring to consciousness'…
(as if that were a dirty word).
Some just keep asking, *Why?*

Without the divine, the imagination,
the grief, the struggle,
life is two-dimensional.
One foot drags after the other,
without meaning.

I lived like that once.
I couldn't go on.

What if the symptoms of my illness
are trying to heal me?

There's nothing worse
than meaningless pain
and meaningless suffering.

———

Once we find the right question
we soon realize
the answer lies in the
unconscious.
Question and answer are two sides of one
thought once we find the right questions.

Stand in the middle.
Let suffering pass through.
Let joy pass through.

Do not identify,
as though there is
nothing but suffering,
nothing but joy.

Yes, there is joy.
Yes, there is suffering.
Say, *I suffer.*
I can *go through this*
and learn what is to be learned.

Stand in the middle,
knowing the suffering will pass,
knowing the joy will pass.

22

Living with Paradox

Most of us have grown up in a culture that divides things into two piles, into dualities: spirit or matter, feminine or masculine, alive or dead, male or female, adult or child, good or bad, light or dark, joyful or painful. We believe things cannot belong in both piles.

In other cultures, this assumption is not experienced as true. What if we were to suspend our belief in it for a while? What if we were to consider the possibility that things are light *and* dark, good *and* bad, joyful *and* painful, spirit *and* matter? We might learn to entertain the notion of paradox, the holding as true of two apparently contradictory ideas, facts, beliefs, or observations at the same time. In so doing, we shall be more able to experience the richness of life, the truth of its beautiful complexity.

—J.M.

We learn to live
in paradox,
in a world where
two apparently exclusive views
are held at the same time.

In this world,
rhythms of paradox are circuitous,
slow, born of feeling
rising from the thinking heart.

Many sense such a place exists.
Few talk or walk from it.

In feminine consciousness,
spiritual and physical
are two aspects of one whole.
This paradox defies
the logic of prose,
demands metaphor, the poet's leap.
Frogs among lilypads
leap from leaf to leaf.

Intimacy reveals our deepest anguish.

———

The paradox of life and death
returns in a new form
at each new spiral of growth.
If we accept this,
we are not torn apart
by opposites.

So what is the rose in the fire?
It is soul
suffering
in the fire
of physical pain and passion.
It is spirit
languishing
as it descends
into physical limitation.
It is matter
ascending towards spirit.
It is the creation
of subtle body.
It is time
in timelessness.
It is light
in matter.

Soulmaking is
allowing eternal essence
to live and experience the outer world
through all the senses
—seeing, smelling, hearing, tasting, touching—
so that soul grows during its time on earth.

Soulmaking is
constantly confronting the paradox
that an eternal being is dwelling
in a temporal body.
That's why it suffers.
That's why it learns by heart.

———

Soul hears with eternal ears,
sees with eternal eyes,
smells with eternal nose.
Yet, having no tongue
other than the transitory language
of the body,
it learns to speak in metaphor.

Birth is the death of the life
we have known;
death, the birth of the life
we have yet to live.

23

Delighting in Play &
Imagination

If play is the work of the soul, imagination is its language. In order to be playful, we need to be in a trustworthy environment where we and those around us respect our vulnerabilities.

Loving parents create places in which their children can play safely. We, too, can provide these so that our playful energies can emerge. Play and imagination are the raw material of adult self-expression in the arts. Children don't need to be talented to enjoy painting or dancing; they do it because they enjoy it. Adults do not need talent either, just a willingness to let go of set ideas about what it means to express themselves in the arts.

The world of play and imagination invites us to let go of expectations and to open up spontaneous creativity in which unexpected wisdom and delight can emerge.

—J.M.

Most of us have forgotten how to play,
forgotten the joy of creativity.
Without joy, we run from pain.
Without creativity, we run from emptiness.
The faster we run, the more severe our
addictions.
We cannot face our nothingness,
the ultimate anguish of living a life knowing
who we are not,
not who we are.

———

Allow the body to play.
Give it space.
Let it make whatever movements
it wants to make.
Just as a dream is an invitation
to the unconscious,
so releasing your body
into spontaneous movement or play
is an invitation to the unconscious.

Seeing is looking with the eyes.
Perceiving is looking
with the eyes of the imagination.

————

The images we take in
are the nutrients of our subtle body.

A gift of the feminine,
metaphor transforms,
crosses from one state to another,
connects psyche and soma.

———

Without metaphor,
culture, dreams, illness, and religion
have no meaning.
Drugs, sports, sex may revive metaphor
for a few hours before flatness
settles in again.
Life without metaphor is intolerable.

To be childlike is
to be spontaneous,
to live in the moment—
concentrated, imaginative, creative.

———

Your images are a picture
of your spiritual condition.

To turn the tomb into a womb,
move with the imagination.

———

We all want to play.
Play lives close to the imagination.
Every minute is new
because something new is constantly happening.
In a relationship, we each need to say,
Let's see how we can play.
Without this, we die.
It doesn't take money.
Just a long leap of faith.

Food and metaphor:
both feed our bodysoul;
both deserve discernment.

How long shall we go on
feeding ourselves
poisoned food and poisoned images?

———

To live a rich life,
we have to be in contact
with our inner world.

24

Beyond Power & Patriarchy

Both *men and women* suffer when power is exercised for its own sake by rule- and authority-bound women and men. Powermongers usually win their own games; they are operating on home territory. To go beyond power and the structures that support it usually involves quietly stepping aside. We do not step aside to disengage but to evolve creative alternatives to power struggles.

We may not be able to do as much as we would like about the way things turn out on sociopolitical battlegrounds, that often require well-coordinated strategies involving many people. However, we can certainly begin with ourselves. We do not have to react in kind. We can learn to choose how we want to respond.

Who are your inner powermongers? What do they say? How do they keep the rules?

—J.M.

Don't blame anyone out there.
You have been treated with power,
and you treat others
as you have been treated.
Have courage:
face the power in yourself.

———

If we have been tyrannized,
we can be fairly sure
we're tyrannizing
someone else—
at least ourselves,
perhaps our bodies.
As we were treated,
so we treat ourselves and others.

In a patriarchy
everything is split.
It's *either or.*
In the feminine realm,
it's *both and.*

———

Living by principles
is not
living your own life.

Men have not escaped
the bludgeoning of the patriarchy.

————

Patriarchy isn't "men"
and isn't only found in men.

The move from power to love
involves immense suffering.

———

Recognizing the difference
between power and love is difficult
if we were raised in a home
where power was disguised as love.

She inherited their beauty and intelligence.
Her mother groomed her to queenhood,
acquainted her
with Yves St. Laurent, Chanel, Harvard,
with the best princes Oxford could offer.
She carried her crown on her regal head—
performed meticulously,
smiled at the right times, wept at the right,
knew when to raise lashes and when to lower.

She did not prosper with the princes;
she became queen of Wall Street,
regal in pinstriped suit and heels.
Always, she carried her insignia,
her black briefcase full of papers, pills, and salve
for headaches, constipation, psoriasis.

And in her chrome and glass apartment,
before she went to bed,
she turned off her computer and stereo,
turned off her rheostat lights,
turned on her electric blanket.

She heard her mother crooning
Old Mother Hubbard,
She went to the cupboard
To give her poor doggie a bone...

She dreamed a computer
was printing out musical scores,
printing each note as a hole
through which she heard
the music for which she yearned.

An unconscious father's daughter
colludes with the lies of patriarchy.

We often repeat
the pattern of our own birth
each time life requires us to move
into new awareness.

25

Practicing Presence

Being present invites us to set aside comparison of our situation with another's, to set aside anticipation and rehearsal of future statements or actions, to set aside memories that interfere with or misinterpret the present moment. Being present invites us to be fully committed to the moment while not being attached to controlling what is not fully under our control: the outcome of whatever is happening right now.

Being present invites us to set aside judgment yet still retain discernment, to set aside sympathy yet hold to empathy, to set aside power yet be responsible for influence. It invites us to bring head, heart, and body into this moment.

—J.M.

The feminine
was, is, and shall be.
It lives in the eternal now.

———

If we could allow the pace of our meetings
to slow down to the pace of our hearts,
we might find genuine understanding.

The feminine mystery lives now.
Its energies are concentrated
on what is happening in this moment:
the scent of wet pine,
a hesitant hand.
The feminine does not save itself
for some glorious moment
in the future,
does not grieve over a lost moment
in the past.
It holds nothing back.
Now is all there is.

Oh sometimes, of course, the soul
enjoys homemade bread and jam,
and sex.

And when you dwell on a candle
in waking or dreaming,
dwell with all of you:
with gut,
with feeling,
with spirit,
with breath,
with mind!
And yes, all the senses
if you're really into it.

You go out
and the moment breaks.
But take it anyway,
knowing that it will break.

When one person in a room is more conscious,
the consciousness of all in the room changes.
If one person in a family is becoming conscious,
everyone in the family changes—
for better or for worse.

We go to great lengths
not to hear our inner voices.
If there's nobody home
we have to hang on for dear life.
Only when there is presence
can we let go.

We suffer but we also know
the joy of seeing that tree, that tree!
There! Look!
We know we're here,
present in the moment!
We give; we receive—
continual flow.

When we face death,
if we've lived life,
we'll be ready.
If we haven't lived it,
never been here,
never been present,
we'll be terrified;
our whole life will have been
an absence.

We shall have missed it.
Well, by heaven,
I don't intend to miss mine.

Femininity is Being
that knows its bone truth.

26

Trusting Deeper Processes

To *believe we understand* all the inner and outer forces in our lives is rather like believing we can understand ocean currents by observing the surface of the water. We all know that there are forces that we do not understand at work in our lives. Some people trust them; some distrust them; some believe them to be divine intervention; others simply live with not understanding them.

What are your own beliefs? Are there other views you might consider?

—J.M.

Conscious femininity gives us
the courage to trust in the moment
without knowing what the goal is.

———

Distilling the truth of the image
is
the work,
a work
that is never finished.

I get up in the morning
to write in my journal.
While I wait for coffee, I wash a sweater.
Good suds! I might as well wash another.
While I'm trying to find it,
I find some soiled scarves
and, by heaven, there's the letter
I couldn't find six months ago.
I put the scarves to soak,
and water my plants.
And trying to find my good stationery
to reply to the old letter,
I find bills I have forgotten to pay
and then I decide to dance.
And I see the mess I'm creating.
So much to do.

Look at their beauty—
women for the first time
finding their sexuality,
men beginning
to know what sexuality is—
they are seeing the beauty
of their shadow,
at sixty-five or seventy.

Now that's grief—
but it's better to find it late
than not at all.
And, I tell you,
grief can open your heart
to incredible love.

———

Outer events are
not important.
Our response to them
is what matters.
It matters to them.

We spend years
building our lives on rotten foundations.

It takes years
to build new foundations
for a new life.

———

Where can I find an hour a day?
To turn away from duty,
to release that energy
into something creative for myself
is like being tossed into a washing machine.
Can I really believe
I am worth an hour a day?
Am I, who have given my life to others,
selfish enough to take one hour a day
to find myself?

27

Body-Soul Resonance

When two things vibrate at the same frequency, they resonate with each other. We, too, have experienced resonance within us: moments when everything in us said *yes* to someone or to something—an embrace, a piece of music, a new opportunity, an exquisite scene. Or moments when everything in us said *no*! These are occasions of body-soul resonance.

You might ask yourself: Do I have to wait for these occasional moments to experience this? Or might I begin to feel and trust this body-soul resonance in my daily life?

—J.M.

Whether we know or not,
our cells know
the love or lack of love
that comes toward us.

———

The earth is screaming.
Our bodies are in trouble.
Matter wants to be redeemed.

A mother who is out of touch
with her own body
cannot give her baby
the sense of harmony with self and universe
fundamental to a later sense of totality.

———

If we are robbed
of our feminine birthright
we are not here.
Our body is not here.

If we are whole,
we resonate
physically, psychically.
Our soul is incarnate.

Abandoned souls
bring themselves forth
whether we work
with ourselves or not.
They seem insatiable because we fail
to understand their language.

When we connect with our souls,
we connect with the soul
of every human being.
We resonate with all living things.
That's where healing is.

Conscious femininity is aware
of the energy in rock, bird, tree, sunset,
aware of living in the world soul.
The body is attuned, concentrated, alive,
open, receptive, alert,
aware in the marrow
of the harmony of the universe.

28

Rites of Passage

I f *we had lived in another time,* we would have passed through life passages with rituals different from those we have (or do not have) now. Puberty, a first sexual experience, becoming an adult, childbirth, the loss of a loved one, illness, the taking on of authority vested in us by age: these transitions from one phase of our lives into another are intense but sadly and too often noted only in passing and half-consciously in our time.

Perhaps it is only in retrospect that we recognize some of our rites of passage. However, we can still remember and celebrate them. And we can be more aware of how we approach them in the future—for ourselves, for others, and for new generations who might once again benefit from having these rites of passage overtly acknowledged.

—J.M.

Transitions are hell.
Our beloved dies or leaves
and we are alone.
That is hell.
It is also time to grow.

Converse alone with body, with soul.
Their wisdom is what we need for wholeness.
Their wisdom makes clear
what is real, what is illusion.
Their wisdom strips false pride.
Their wisdom makes us human.

Each hell burns off more illusions.
We go into the fire, die,
and are reborn.

Rites of passage
are inner and outer,
body and psyche at limit.
We journey through
the labyrinth of our souls.
The mystery
lures us into death,
which leads us into life.

———

Rites of passage are accompanied
by image.
The image partakes of spirit and matter,
belongs to neither,
is possessed by neither.
The image is the map
for the new country.
We hold the tension
until the new image comes;
if we do not, the gold is lost,
the initiation fails.

Rites of passage are accompanied
by surrender.
We let ourselves drop
into our charged body.
Soul surrenders to spirit.
Our relationship to ourselves
and to the world is recreated.

———

Rites of passage are accompanied
by tenacity.
The tunnel of death and rebirth
demands supreme effort,
demands holding on
without orientation
until the light.

Rites of passage are accompanied
by concentration.
Concentration directs energy
toward consciousness,
learns to take direction
from within,
discovers a world with its own order.
Every minute is new.
Every minute is now.

———

Rites of passage are accompanied
by preparation and purification:
a bath,
a garment,
a dance,
a sacrifice....

Rites of passage are accompanied
by strength.
Possession blinds.
We grow strong enough
to surrender
free of possession
by instinct or spirit.

———

Rites of passage are accompanied
by intensity.
Intensity brings us
to the moment
when the mystery bursts through.

Change and flux:
in the decay of the old
and the birth of the new,
the rhythm of the feminine.

29

The Shadow

W*hen we stand in the light,* we cast a shadow. Light and shade are to each other as breathing in is to breathing out. Some aspects of ourselves are in the light, visible to us and others. Other aspects, positive and negative, are in shadow, unseen by us, even when seen by others. These are parts of ourselves that have been neglected, disowned, forgotten, judged, unrecognized, or undeveloped.

Some of the ways we can glimpse what is in the psychological shade include noting what we idealize or denigrate in others; recognizing our uneasiness about others' perceptions of us (good and bad); and paying attention to our bodies, where shadow can sometimes reside as a physical symptom (an aching back, a pain in the stomach).

Our shadow is an infinite reservoir of energy. Learning to recognize and to take responsibility for our shadow qualities gives us more choice in responding consciously and creatively to the possibilities life offers us.

—J.M.

The shadow is anything
we are sure we are not;
it is part of us we do not know,
sometimes do not want to know,
most times do not want to know.
We can hardly bear to look.

Look.
It may carry the best of the life
we have not lived.

If we're ever to get along with our mates,
we have to deal with our shadow.
How can we have intimacy with another
when we lie to ourselves?

————

If we allow ourselves to receive,
to be ravished by the irrational,
we are compelled to face our own evil.
Trust takes on new dimension:
In knowing our own darkness,
we know what another's darkness can release.
We learn to forgive and to love.
There we don't know
from moment to moment
what will happen next.
That is God's country.

Once we've recognized our shadow,
once we've accepted it
as part of who we are,
and begun to civilize it,
we are no longer judgmental of others.

———

Intuitive people are blessed and cursed.
They are confounded by possibilities,
driven this way and that by what might be.
They are rarely in the present,
never quite filling their bodies.

Their bodies become vulnerable
to all the pain in their environment.
Through osmosis they pick up
others' unconscious garbage.
Intuitive people are blessed and cursed.

Repressed energy returns
to haunt us
in symbols and symptoms.

———

God preserve me
from being reduced to my shadow.

Trying to be a god or a goddess
all week
can flip us into being an animal
all weekend.

———

Our shadow may contain
the best of ourselves.

How the energy in the body
has been caged!
Released (which happens quickly),
there is danger in accepting it
without reserve
as a saving grace.

It is shadow.
Do not embrace it
as a long-lost sister.

Recognize.
Don't act impulsively.
Maintain healthy suspicion.
To live out is not to integrate.
Chew and digest.

Don't use
a whip that will kill its spirit.
Put a rider on the wild horse.

To claim our unlived parts
is to stand in our own shoes.
crumpled as they may be.

———

We cannot kill energy.
It goes underground.
It always rises again
in another, strange way.

The Self
pushes the neglected forward
for recognition.
Do not disregard it.
It holds energy
of highest value.
It is the gold in the dung.
Do not disregard the dung.

30

Coming to Love

T*he kind of loving* into which we are invited in the following pages may be familiar or unfamiliar. It certainly goes beyond personal attachment and physical attraction. This love walks in with an open heart, open hands, open eyes, and open mind. This love is not blind to human flaws in itself or in others. Rather it invites us to embrace others with full awareness of both the light and the dark.

Can we experience this kind of love for ourselves, for others, from others?

—J.M.

Whatever their outcome,
the profound relationships in our lives
give us the riches of loving.
That wealth is the only wealth
that means anything in the end.

———

The mystery of God touches us—
or does not—
in the smallest details:
giving a strawberry,
with love;
receiving a touch,
with love;
sharing the snapdragon red
of an autumn sunset,
with love.

Only by opening ourselves to inner reality
do we open
to the possibility of love.
Action and choice are needed:
we can accept;
we can reject;
we can withdraw.

We cannot make it happen.
Love chooses us.

————

He is.
I am.
Tough stuff!

Imagine BEING love.

———

Real love happens
when soul in the body
meets soul in the body.
Not in that disembodied world of spirit
where we want to be perfect,
but in life,
where we're changing the diapers
of one we love who is dying,
swabbing the lips,
doing things we never thought we could do.
Stripped of all pride, of everything unreal,
we have no false modesty.
Where soul meets soul, that is love.

One day you shall be able to say,
I am.
I am loved.
I can receive love.
I do love myself.
I do love.
Perhaps today.

31

Trusting the Mystery

The *mystery* this section contemplates is not the kind found in a detective novel. Rather, it is the gatekeeper of the sacred. To dispel this kind of mystery with too harsh a light—to explain away everything about our dream, about love, about commitments—is to tear down the gate and allow sacred ground to be trampled. Mystery keeps us humble, keeps our rationality aware of its ignorance.

Sustaining awareness of the mystery of what it is to be human, of what our dreams are, of what certain piercing moments "mean," reminds us what a wonderfully small part of a larger life flow we are.

As you reflect on these pages, you might ask yourself where you experience a sense of mystery in your life.

—J.M.

Why should we have more faith
in an amaryllis bulb
than in ourselves?
We know, perhaps,
that the amaryllis lives
by an inner law
with which we have lost touch
in ourselves.

The blossom dies;
with rest and darkness,
another bloom will come
we know, next year.
In this place of the goddess,
we accept birth and death.

When we listen to the amaryllis,
resonate with its silence,
its eternal stillness, we find ourselves
at the heart of the mystery.

Consciousness changes the perceived.
Science knows this.
Psychology is slower to believe.

———

I trust there is a healing process
going on in my unconscious.
If I can keep in touch with it,
my life flows forward;
I constantly open to what
I could never have imagined.

If you watch a caterpillar
you might catch the moment
when the crawling stops.
Delicate membranes attach to a twig,
old skin is shed, pupal skin hardens.

The caterpillar chooses the food
the butterfly will need,
chooses the exact space
to later spread its wings.
Without the space,
the wings would never fly.

The chrysalis is essential.
It is the twilight zone,
a precarious world
between past and future.

The grub will not emerge
as a high class caterpillar.
Does it know
what will go on inside?
Does it prepare
for the winged beauty
that slowly and painfully emerges,
that will live by a new set of laws?

If you're a happy carrot,
why wouldn't you remain a happy carrot?
If you're happy, and your life is mostly joy,
why would you want to be conscious?

Few of us come to consciousness
without great pain;
something unbearable
has happened.

Don't try to take others
out of carrothood.
You'll be responsible
for trying to make them conscious,
and that is misuse of power.
Some people are happy carrots.
God bless them!

———

Unconscious means
not conscious!

Our stillpoint at center:
the psychic pendulum swings
through to the left.
We say,
I despair,
but I am not despair.
This shall pass.
It swings through to the right.
We say,
I am in love,
hopelessly in love.
This too shall pass.

———

As we once entered the world,
so we still enter
each new spiral of growth.

Until consciousness intercedes.

Once we are in the flow
of our life's river,
we experience synchronicity.
Outer and inner
become
much the same.

32

Listening to My Soul

Howwever we define "soul," we know when we encounter it. We don't have to ask. We are suffused with it.

Unless we invite our soul into our lived experience, we can miss its gifts to us in daily life—whether in an intimate encounter with another, in nature, in the arts, in spiritual setting or through our bodies, in illness and in healing and in health.

Here we are reminded to listen closely, for the soul often speaks in a whisper, easily drowned out in the busyness of daily life.

—J.M.

As long as we are determined
to move at our swift, logical pace,
our child remains hidden.
The soul-bird put away
in a dark box in childhood
needs time, needs silence
to learn to trust again.

If you see yourself
as no one worth looking at;
if you believe you are
not worth listening to;
if your parents didn't find
you worth looking at,
worth listening to;
if they told you,
That's not what you saw,
not what you heard,
not what you think,
you cannot trust yourself,
you are lost.

Don't look to others to find you,
to love and take care of you now.
You'll suck them dry.

No one out there is responsible.
Go back and find your soul.
Be mother and father to yourself,
Until the divine parents arrive.

In his eighties, he was my analyst.
I had been in England
seeing him for six months,
and was still trying to be efficient.
On Christmas Eve I learned my dog,
who was in Canada, had been killed.
I decided not to waste my evening session
talking about my dog.
I arrived as organized as usual.
At the end, he sat quietly,
then asked me what was wrong.
Nothing, I said, as I put on my coat.
You have not been here, he said.
I told him my dog was dead.
He wept. Wept over my dog.
Asked me how I could waste Christmas Eve
chattering when my soul animal had just died.
Suddenly his weeping made me feel
what I was doing to my soul.
We wept together.
That's when my analysis began.

Loss of soul connection,
loss of connection to our femininity,
may be the real cause of our anguish.
If we have no bridge
to the depths that drive us,
our rational attempts
to correct our situation
are merely Band-aids.

———

Shame was put upon you.
It is not yours.
Your soul need not
be limited by shame.

Our souls cry out
from underneath the rubble of our lives,
like children who have not known love,
children begging us to say,
You are not alone.
I love you.

———

In living the abandoned child
within herself
the woman becomes pregnant
with herself.

When we identify with our childish side
we say,
I was always a victim.
I will always be a victim
and it's all my parents' fault,
then walk around with a hangdog face
the rest of our lives.

When we gather our child into our arms,
we say,
My parents were victims of a culture,
as were their parents and their parents.
I shall not be a victim.
I shall take responsibility for my own life.
I shall live creatively.
I shall live now.

The soul may go into hiding,
but it does not die.

———

The soul
is,
present tense,
now.
Dancing in the flames.

Sooner or later we find her.
In dreams, she appears, that child,
(never at the beginning,
never at the beginning—
we would go crazy with grief).
She is starving in a pile of garbage,
in a basement under the basement.
Somebody tried to kill her.
Frightened, she ran downstairs.
She may even accuse you.

She is the age she was
when she fled.
And she must be fed.

One hour a day, let her play,
let her sing, let her dance,
let her be with her dreams.
Feed her.
She will grow strong and beautiful.

33

Timely Sacrifices

I f *we are connected* to others through caring, friendship, or love, we know what it is to make sacrifices on a daily basis. We regularly set aside immediate personal wishes for the common good or to accommodate other legitimate needs.

At certain times, we also hear inner calls—to sacrifice old ways, old beliefs, old attachments, old attitudes. These sacrifices are more challenging because usually they carry with them no promise, no guarantee, no contract.

We need courage to open up heart, mind, and body to something as yet unformed. All we know is that the old way is no longer working and that we have no choice but to embrace the unknown.

—J.M.

Most of us are dragged
toward wholeness.
We do not understand
the breakdown of what has gone before.
We do not understand.
We cling to the familiar,
refuse to make necessary sacrifices,
refuse to give up habitual lives,
resist our growth.
We do not understand rebirth,
do not accept the initiation rites.
Most of us are dragged
toward wholeness.

———

If we must surrender a close bond,
we need to learn
to sacrifice the relationship
without sacrificing the love.

Once you have explored the depths,
don't wallow in them.
It's not only boring,
it's destructive.
Let grace enter.
It brings with it
a new understanding of love.

———

Out of the chrysalis,
in its first moment,
perhaps in first flight,
the butterfly voids
a drop, frequently red.

We, too, may sacrifice
a drop of the past,
turn to the future,
unfold our wings,
and say,
I am.

Periods of renunciation
are the initiations in life
when we realize
God is not running a day care center.

———

Sometimes only with distance
may the depth of the root
of a relationship become apparent.
The plant may be cut off
almost to the ground
and still, with care,
rejuvenate.

Through failures, symptoms, problems,
we are prodded
to renounce attachments,
redundant now.
With the breakdown of what has gone before,
the possibility of rebirth comes.

We fall into old habits:
afraid to lose old friends,
afraid to lose our relationship,
afraid to lose our job,
afraid to make a fool of ourselves.

Friends say,
You never were like this.
I don't like you like this.

Your mate says,
You're not the person I married.
I don't like this one.
Why don't you stop?

You say,
This is who I am!
Your mate says,
If this is who you are, good luck.
I didn't promise to live with this person.

Most of us can only let so much go at a time.

Simplifying is the most elegant of tasks
in our cluttered culture.

34

Initiation into the Deep Feminine

*I*n *these pages,* we find the story of one woman's unexpected initiation into a deeper, embodied understanding of feminine energies. Fear, courage, pain, joy, and openness accompany such initiations.

As you follow this journey, you might reflect on the phases of initiation: departure, loss of an old identity and psychic death accompanied often by physical suffering, insight into new possibilities, rebirth, and reintegration of the new understandings and new identity into the familiar world.

Where do your experiences intersect, parallel, or contrast with these? How have you been initiated into your deeper knowing? How might you be more courageous and more open to the initiatory experiences in your life?

—J.M.

One winter night
I was alone.
I needed a taxi.
I raised my arm
but the taxis didn't stop.
I was not forthright enough.

I walked through the snow
in the dark to where I was going.
Something had to change.
I knew I would buy
a ticket to India
and hoped I might
encounter God
in an ashram in Pondicherry.

I stay first in Delhi.
Terror becomes my gasoline.

Hands grasp at me—
crippled beggars,
black market hustlers
demanding American dollars,
professional lovers
assuring me they are second
only to Africans.

And two tiny waifs, older, here, than I.
Each morning they wait at the entrance.
All day they cling to my dress.
Each evening I sew up the seams.

I brush kisses with a cow,
step in her pancake.
People shout,
Good evening
in the morning.
I know something is wrong
when I shout back,
Good evening.

She picked up a bag of bones.
I've often thought of that woman.
She asked me if I was alone.
I said *Yes* and fainted dead away.
She picked up the bones from the street,
put them in a taxi, and took them with her.
She had no idea what she had.
She took me to her hotel,
determined I was going home.
I knew I had to stay.

I teem with elusive images.
In this monsoon season, the hotel balcony teems
with drenched crows
croaking *Nevermore*
and the bathtub is alive
with cockroaches.
I fall on the tile floor.
How long I am there,
I do not know.

I awake on the ceiling,
soul looking down at body
caked in dry vomit and excrement.
Helpless, still,
it takes a breath.
Poor dummy, I think,
Don't you know you're dead?
And give it a kick.

I watch it take another breath.
Will they burn it?
Will they send it home?
Then I remember my dog, trusting, faithful,
waiting for me to return.
I look at my body, trusting, faithful,
waiting for me to return.

It takes another breath.
I come down, move in.
We drag ourselves to the little bed.

I do my best to take care of her.

There is no one to phone,
no one to visit,
nothing to do.
All escapes cut.

In this descent into hell
for days, perhaps nine,
I lie in this narrow hotel bed reading
Shakespeare's sonnets,
the New Testament
and my passport
aloud.

On the tenth day,
the worst illness passes,
I venture to the lobby.
I sit on the couch writing a letter.
A woman in gold-trimmed sari,
fat arm warm and black,
squeezes between me
and the end of the couch.

I pull away
to make room to write.
She cuddles against me.
I move again. She moves.
I smile. She smiles.
She speaks no English.

By the time I finish my letter,
we are both at the other end,
her body pressed to mine.

The next day, still fearful of outside,
I return. And she returns.
The dignified game goes on.
And does for days.

One morning, as I am returning
to my room, he steps up.
You're all right now, he says.
You were dying.
I sent my wife to sit with you.
I knew the warmth of her body
would bring you back to life.
She won't need to come again.

I am ravished:
stench of urine
and perfume of jasmine;
flies in a baby's eyes
and a blaze of red silk;
screams of a beaten dog
and sweetness of a sitar
on this summer night.

The taxi driver's enigmatic smile,
the narrow roadway,
the featureless fields:
I hope we are on our way to the caves.
I see a dog with a canary yellow eye.
I see a cow with turquoise horns.
I see an elephant, translucent pink.

The driver is not disturbed.
He is conjuring ways to get me
into the front seat.
It is Krishna's birthday. Do you want to go?
Yes.
Singing, he swings the taxi into the ditch
and through the fields.

Four pairs of hands take
sandals, camera, purse, belt.
The faces of twenty men regard me.
I never thought I would die this way.
They bow in low salaam and straighten
until green eyes meet fiery black.
I will not faint.

They raise me above their heads.
Chanting, they carry me,
lay me gently on the ground.

The priest places grass in my mouth,
prays over me.
He divides my grass among the men.
They eat it as if it is holy.
They raise me, place me on an altar,
chant and dance slow around.

They salaam and carry me
away from holy ground,
give me sandals, camera, purse, and belt.
The driver reappears,
smiling his nonchalant smile.
We bounce across the fields.

In dark arms and dusty field,
I hear Her.
I know the grass between my lips is holy.
I know my milkmaid's body,
Krishna's bride.

*She returned
triumphant and transformed:*
it was not that way at all.

When I passed through Amsterdam,
I was shattered by noise.
I saw a woman in boots
with yellow hair, pink lipstick,
and turquoise eye shadow.
*She must be going
to Krishna's birthday.*

Why did you go to India?
Each time I went for analysis,
he asked me again.

*You must be going senile.
You ask every time I come.*

*And every time you give me a different answer.
When I was a brigadier in India,
we had a hard time with some of the soldiers.
They didn't want to fight.*

*They put seeds in their eyes,
to make them blind,
and then they were sent home.
You think about that.*

I've been taking seeds out of my eyes
for sixteen years.

———

In ancient rites
we would have met the mystery
in an underground passage,
an inner surrender
to our deepest eroticism.

Giving up desire,
in aloneness and despair
we would have surrendered
to what we believed was death.
We would have known the coming together
of matter and spirit,
of human and divine:
a love marriage with the god.

We cannot go back.
We cannot go back to the ancient mysteries.
Yet we can make the journey
below and back again.
We can know the light in our darkness,
can find again, within our body,
the sacred mystery.

Every night I dreamt
I was falling.

One night I landed.
Landed in strange terrain.
Frightened, paralyzed,
I felt around with my fingers,
and thought what I felt was sand.

It wasn't sand.
It was feathers,
and I was seated
on the wings of the Holy Spirit.

That dream changed my life.

In my dream,
I was a priestess
and had prepared
the altar for great celebration.
The flowers were almost in place,
the roses almost in the center
of the sunlit altar.
(I could not make the roses fit
within the light.)
A shadow the shape of a cross
came through a window.

An old man came to me and said,
Your hymns will never rise to heaven
until you clean up your mess in the basement.

But there's no basement in this temple, I said.
That's the problem: there is, he replied.

Down the rotting old steps we went
and found a slimy lagoon.
A water wheel,
joining basement to temple, lay still.

A huge serpent writhed,
trying and failing and trying again
to center its head on the wheel.
It knew its task was to turn the wheel—

quiet, rhythmic—with its head.

I tried to move the wheel towards the serpent
and it struck.
The old man pulled me out of danger,
You can't move so fast
She doesn't trust you.
Hasten slowly;
you will make her your friend.

For twenty years,
the wheel has creaked but turned;
The lagoon, fresh;
the serpent, Sophia;
the roses, not yet in place.

REFERENCES

Woodman, Marion. *Addiction to Perfection: The Still Unravished Bride*. Toronto: Inner City Books, 1982.

_____. *Conscious Femininity: Interviews with Marion Woodman*. Toronto: Inner City Books, 1993.

_____. *Dreams: Language of the Soul* (cassette recording no. A131). Boulder, CO: Sounds True Recordings, 1991.

_____. *Emily Dickinson and the Demon Lover* (cassette recording no. A225). Boulder, CO: Sounds True Recordings, 1993.

_____. *Holding the Tension of the Opposites* (cassette recording no. A138). Boulder, CO: Sounds True Recordings, 1991.

_____. *Leaving My Father's House: A Journey to Conscious Femininity* (with Kate Danson, Mary Hamilton, and Rita Greer Allen). Boston: Shambhala, 1992.

_____. *The Owl Was a Baker's Daughter: Obesity, Anorexia Nervosa and the Repressed Feminine*. Toronto: Inner City Books, 1980.

_____. *The Pregnant Virgin: A Process of Psychological Transformation*. Toronto: Inner City Books, 1985.

_____. *The Ravaged Bridegroom: Masculinity in Women*. Toronto: Inner City Books, 1990.

_____. *Rolling Away the Stone* (cassette recording no. A095). Boulder, CO: Sounds True Recordings, 1989.

_____. *The Stillness Shall Be the Dancing: Feminine and Masculine in Emerging Balance* (cassette recording). College Station, TX: Texas A&M University Press, 1994.

Woodman, Marion and Dickson, Elinor. *Dancing in the Flames: The Dark Goddess in the Transformation of Consciousness*. Boston: Shambhala, 1996.

Alphabetical Index

The following works have been cited and are abbreviated as follows in the text:

The references from which the selection has been taken are listed after the abbreviation so that those familiar with Marion Woodman's work may revisit material of value to them and so that those less familiar may quickly find entry through a particular perspective that touches them.

Without our body we cannot speak truthfully   HTO
Write dreams down   DLS
Your images are a picture   RAS

Index by Reference

Conscious Femininity

Dreams: Language of the Soul

If the dream uses a symbol
If we are full of rage
If we have been tyrannized
If you don't believe
If you paint
If you see yourself
If you're a happy carrot
In her dream
Masculinity is in men and women
Once you are in the flow
Once you dance for a year
Once we know what the dream world is
Patriarchy isn't "men"
The shadow is anything
Sleep brings the body into balance
Sooner or later we find her
Stand in the middle
There's nothing worse
To live a rich life
To sit in a chair and analyze
We cannot take in the dream
We fall into old habits
We spend years
What on earth is that person
When the path is blocked

Oh sometimes, of course, the soul
On Friday I sent the clothes
Our banquet of dreams is spread each night
So if you dream of Isis—fine
To turn the tomb into a womb
We cannot kill the energy
We project god and goddess out
When she comes in a dream
Your images are a picture

The Stillness Shall Be the Dancing
Any woman who takes herself seriously
A compulsive relationship
Consciousness changes the perceived
Do you think I have a father complex?
Femininity is Being
Food and metaphor
God preserve me
How many people do you know
Hypocrisy, sentimentality, distraction
If we are depending on our partner
If we could allow the pace of our meetings
If you find yourself
Intimacy reveals our deepest anguish
Once we find the right question
Our shadow may contain

Marion Woodman, Ph.D.

Marion Woodman, Ph.D. (Hon.) is a widely read and acclaimed author, leader in feminine development research and teaching, and a Jungian analyst. She is the author of many widely respected books that bridge the fields of analytical psychology and feminine psychology, including *Addiction to Perfection* (Inner City Books, Toronto, 1982), *The Pregnant Virgin* (Inner City Books, 1985), and *Leaving My Father's House* (co-authored) (Shambhala, 1992). Her other well-known works include *The Owl Was a Baker's Daughter* (Inner City Books, 1980), *The Ravaged Bridegroom* (1990), *Conscious Femininity* (Inner City Books, 1992) and her latest, co-authored work, *Dancing in the Flames* (Shambhala, 1996). Her works have been published in over fifteen editions and translated into nine languages. She is also the author of many articles and audio tapes, including a set of tapes on dreams, *Dreams: Language of the Soul*, which are available from Sounds True Recordings.

Marion Woodman has presented at or led over two hundred workshops and conferences and well over three hundred lectures in Canada, the United States, and Europe. Most recently, she has been leading workshops on fairytales with her friend, poet and leader in the men's movement, Robert Bly, and a series of excellent videotapes of their work *"Bly and Woodman on Men and Women"* is available from Applewood, Belleville, Canada.

She has a graduate degree in English from the University of Western Ontario, London, Ontario and several honorary doctorates including one from her alma mater and one from ITP. Until she became a Jungian analyst, she was a highly popular English and drama teacher at a high school in London, Ontario. She brings her life-long love of literature and drama to her Jungian workshops, writing, and lectures. She has traveled widely and, until recently, spent most summers with family on her island retreat in Georgian Bay in Northern Ontario.

JILL MELLICK, PH.D.

Jill Mellick, Ph.D. is a Jungian-oriented clinical psychologist in private practice and a faculty member of the Institute of Transpersonal Psychology in Palo Alto, California where she directs the Creative Expression Programs.

The author of two books, *The Worlds of P'otsunu: Geronia Cruz Montoya of San Juan Pueblo*, which she co-authored with Jeanne Shutes, Ph.D. and *The Natural Artistry of Dreams: Creative Ways to Bring the Wisdom of Dreams to Waking Life* (Conari Press). A published poet, exhibiting artist, and performing musician, her music appears on Marion's tape: *Emily Dickinson and the Demon Lover.* She has led or co-led workshops in California, her native Australia, and New Mexico. She travels widely, usually observing the use of the arts for psychospiritual purposes, particularly in Greece, Switzerland, Japan, and in Pueblo Indian country in the Southwest.

She and Marion have known each other for many years in many capacities: through Marion's workshops, in many of which Jill has participated; through working together on several projects, through Marion's annual women's retreats at Georgian Bay in Canada at which Jill has been a regular assistant, and through friendship.

Conari Press, established in 1987, publishes books on topics
ranging from spirituality and women's history to sexuality and
personal growth. Our main goal is to publish quality books
that will make a difference in people's lives—both
how we feel about ourselves and how
we relate to one another.

Our readers are our most important resource, and we
value your input, suggestions, and ideas. We'd love to hear
from you—after all, we are publishing
books for you!

For a complete catalog or to be added to our mailing list,
please contact us at:

CONARI PRESS
2550 Ninth Street, Suite 101
Berkeley, California 94710

800-685-9595   Fax 510-649-7190
e-mail Conari@conari.com
www.conari.com